BUILD A PROFITABLE
CONSULTING PRACTICE

Build a Profitable

Consulting Practice

RICHARD LOWE

CONTENTS

See books by Richard Lowe at
https://masterofworlds.com

Get free publishing insights and industry updates at
https://thewritingking.substack.com

For ghostwriting and book coaching services see
https://thewritingking.com

| 1 |

Introduction

During my second semester in college, I arrived late at the twice-annual tradition of registration. To my dismay, the good classes had filled up, and all that remained were a couple of computer courses with funny sounding names. This was long before computers became cool. In fact, I'd never seen one before and only knew about them from science fiction stories.

I didn't want to take a computer class, but nothing else remained, and I had to fill my schedule. I signed up, and by the end of the first day of the first class, I was hooked.

My teacher stood almost 7 feet tall, very knowledgeable and likable. His name was Fred, and after a single semester I knew what I would do with the rest of my life.

Near the end of the semester, Fred gave me my first consulting gig. This involved correcting some bugs in the general ledger programs that ran on a TRS-80 computer. At the time, you couldn't buy a more modern machine. It came with 16KB of memory and two 5 ¼ inch floppy disk drives. I was overconfident, underprepared, and completely naive. I had my eye on the $600 the client offered to complete the job and didn't realize I had no idea how to fix the programs until I'd gotten in too deep.

Looking back on those days, I realize I did everything wrong that I could possibly do wrong. I didn't validate my assumptions, didn't write a statement of work, and didn't terminate the contract when I found myself in over my head.

Now, more than forty years later, I've been part of or managed several hundred consulting projects. Some lasted an hour or two, some required weeks of labor, and others needed teams of 20 people working for months at a time.

I successfully completed virtually all these projects relatively close to budget and almost always on time. I learned there was a certain joy in delivering a high-quality service to a client that met or exceeded the specifications.

Those projects that didn't go well failed in over 90% of the cases because I communicated poorly with the client. Conversely, those projects that succeeded did so primarily because I maintained excellent communication between the client, the implementation team, and myself.

Good communication starts with the sales effort, continues when you write a high-quality statement of work (SOW), and proceeds all the way to the end of the project through meetings, email, video calls, and telephone calls.

Of course, many other factors go into the success or failure of a project. Obviously, a consultant must be competent and understand the service he's selling and must be able to manage and control the chaos that can happen in any activity involving many people.

You must manage change as well. A project that's otherwise going well can get thoroughly torpedoed and sink into the depths if you don't control change properly.

In this book, I'll present many of the lessons I learned about how to manage a project from beginning to end. I'll talk about what makes a project go right and the things that can go wrong.

| 2 |

What is a consulting project?

Most consultants miss the most important thing about consulting: your real product isn't the website you build, the system you implement, or the strategy you develop. Your real product is the experience you create for your client. They'll remember how you made them feel long after they've forgotten the technical details of what you delivered.

Everything else follows from that. When you carry the trust someone placed in you when they handed over their money, when you deliver excellent work within budget and on time, and when you communicate at a high level throughout — clients recommend you. They write glowing testimonials. When their peers need a consultant, they mention your name first. That's how you build a real business.

When you screw up, you get bad reviews or no testimonial at all. You definitely won't get recommendations, and anyone who asks your former client about you will hear either stony silence or a colorful description of your shortcomings. That reputation follows you.

In marketing, nothing beats a personal recommendation from someone people trust. Every position I've held throughout my career started because someone recommended me. During my 14 years as Vice President of Consulting, I landed most of my projects through client recommendations. When I switched sides and started hiring consultants at Trader Joe's, I hired hundreds of them based almost entirely on recommendations.

The point is simple: a consulting project isn't just a transaction. It's the beginning of a reputation — either one that opens doors or one that closes them.

I learned this lesson the hard way during my third consulting project. The client hired me to upgrade their inventory system, and I delivered exactly what they asked for, on time and under budget. The system worked perfectly. But I was so focused on the technical work that I barely communicated with them during the project. When they called with questions, I gave short, technical answers. When they wanted updates, I sent brief emails with minimal detail.

The system ran flawlessly for years, but they never hired me again. When I ran into the project manager at a conference two years later, he told me they'd been happy with my work but felt like I didn't care about their business. That stung because I did care, I just didn't show it.

From that point forward, I made sure every client felt like their project was the most important thing on my plate. I called them regularly, explained things in plain English, and showed genuine interest in their business challenges. My technical skills didn't improve much over the next few years, but my client satisfaction scores went through the roof.

The consulting business is fundamentally about solving problems for people who don't have the time, knowledge, or resources to solve those problems themselves. Sometimes the problem is technical: they need a new database or a mobile app. Sometimes it's strategic: they need to figure out how to enter a new market or restructure their operations. Sometimes it's political: they need an outside voice to say things that insiders can't say without risking their careers.

Your job extends far beyond just solving the problem. You need to solve it in a way that makes the client feel confident, informed, and valued. You need to solve it without creating new problems. And you need to solve it in a way that positions you for the next project.

That last part might sound mercenary, but it's in your client's best interest. If you do good work and they trust you, they'll bring you back when new challenges arise. This saves them the time and risk of finding and vetting new consultants. It saves you the cost of finding new clients. Everybody wins.

The most successful consultants I know treat every project like the beginning of a long-term relationship, not a one-time transaction. They invest time in understanding their client's business, culture, and long-term goals. They look for ways to add value beyond the immediate scope of work. They stay in touch between projects and offer insights when relevant opportunities arise.

This doesn't mean you should pad your bills or extend projects unnecessarily. It means you should think strategically about how your current work sets the stage for future opportunities while delivering exceptional value right now.

The most important point about consulting projects: they're not just about the work you do. They're about the trust you build, the relationships you develop, and the reputation you create. Master those elements, and the technical work becomes much easier to manage.

| 3 |

Statement of work

The statement of work will save your ass more times than you can count. I've seen more consulting projects go sideways because of a bad SOW than any other single factor. Get this document right, and you'll avoid 90% of the headaches that plague other consultants.

Your SOW spells out exactly what you're going to do, when you're going to do it, and what the client will get when you're done. Think of it as the technical blueprint attached to your contract. The contract handles the legal stuff like payment terms and liability. The SOW handles the nuts and bolts of the work.

I learned this lesson during my fourth consulting project. A small manufacturing company hired me to build them a customer database. Simple enough, right? We shook hands on a $3,000 project that should have taken two weeks.

Three months later, I was still working on it. The project had grown to include inventory tracking, sales reporting, automated billing, email integration, and a web portal for customers to check their order status. The client kept saying things like "while you're in there, could you also..." and "it would be really helpful if the system could..."

I was young and stupid and wanted to keep the client happy, so I kept saying yes. By the time I finally delivered something, I'd worked about 200 hours for that original $3,000. That's $15 an hour, less than I could have made flipping burgers.

The client was thrilled with the final system. It did everything they wanted and more. But I was bitter about the whole experience and they could sense it. They never hired me again, and they certainly didn't recommend me to anyone else.

That's when I started writing detailed statements of work for every project, no matter how small.

A good SOW starts with a clear description of the current situation. You want to document exactly what exists today before you change anything. This gives you a baseline and helps prevent misunderstandings later.

Then you describe exactly what the finished project will look like. Don't just say "build a website" or "implement a CRM system." Paint a picture. Walk through scenarios. Describe what users will see and do.

For that manufacturing company, a proper SOW would have said something like: "The customer database will store contact information, purchase history, and payment status for up to 5,000 customers. Users will be able to search by company name, contact name, or phone number. The system will generate three standard reports: monthly sales summary, overdue accounts, and new customer list. The database will run on the client's existing Windows server and integrate with their current QuickBooks installation."

Notice how detailed that is. There's no room for interpretation about what "customer database" means. If the client wants inventory tracking or a web portal, that's a different project with a different SOW.

Your SOW should also spell out what you're not going to do. This sounds negative, but it's critical. Clients have vivid imaginations, and they'll assume your project covers all sorts of things you never intended to deliver.

Using that same example: "This project does not include inventory management, automated billing, email marketing, or web-based customer access. Training will be limited to two hours of basic system operation. Ongoing technical support is not included."

Be brutal about this section. If you don't exclude something explicitly, the client will assume it's included.

Next, lay out your timeline with clear milestones. Don't just say "the project will take four weeks." Break it down: "Week 1: Database design and approval. Week 2: Data entry screens and basic reports. Week 3: Data migration and testing. Week 4: Training and go-live."

Each milestone should have a deliverable that the client can review and approve. This keeps the project moving forward and prevents surprises at the end.

Include your assumptions in the SOW. These are the things you're taking for granted about the project. Maybe you're assuming the client's server has enough disk space. Maybe you're assuming their data is clean and doesn't need extensive cleanup. Maybe you're assuming they'll provide a dedicated contact person who can answer questions quickly.

Write down these assumptions because they will bite you if you don't. I once spent an extra week on a project because the client's "clean" customer database turned out to be a mess of duplicates, missing information, and obsolete records. If I'd included data cleanup in my assumptions, I could have either budgeted time for it or made it the client's responsibility.

Your SOW should nail down exactly what the client needs to provide. This might cover access to systems, sample data, feedback on designs, or dedicated time from key personnel. If the client doesn't hold up their end of the bargain, you need documented proof that the delay isn't your fault.

Finally, build in a change control process. Change is inevitable on any project worth doing, but it doesn't have to destroy your budget or timeline. Your SOW should spell out exactly how changes will be handled.

Something like: "Any changes to the scope of work must be documented in writing and approved by both parties before implementation. Changes may affect the project timeline and budget. Additional work will be billed at $X per hour."

This isn't about being difficult or inflexible. It's about managing expectations and protecting both you and the client from scope creep.

I've written SOWs for projects ranging from $500 website updates to $2 million system implementations. The size doesn't matter. What matters is clarity. A good SOW eliminates confusion, sets clear expectations, and gives you a roadmap for success.

The best SOW is one that's so detailed and clear that someone else could pick it up and complete your project. If you can achieve that level of clarity, you'll avoid most of the problems that sink other consultants.

AI tools can help draft an initial SOW structure quickly — describe the project and ask for a statement of work outline, and you'll get a reasonable starting framework in a few minutes. Use it. But read every word before you send it to a client. AI-generated SOWs include plausible-sounding language that may not match what you actually agreed to, leave out assumptions you need to document, and sometimes contradict themselves across sections. Treat the AI draft as a first pass that needs your expertise applied to it, not a finished document.

| 4 |

Pricing and contracts

Nothing will kill your consulting business faster than bad pricing and weak contracts. I've watched talented consultants go broke because they undercharged for their work or signed contracts that left them exposed when things went wrong.

Your price sends a message about the value of your work. Price too low, and clients assume you're either desperate or incompetent. Price too high without the credentials to back it up, and you won't get hired at all. Find that sweet spot, and you'll attract the right clients who respect your expertise.

When I started consulting, I made the classic rookie mistake of competing on price. I'd submit bids that were 20% lower than my competitors, thinking this would guarantee me the work. Wrong. Half the time, clients assumed my low prices meant low quality and hired someone else anyway. The other half hired me but treated me like a discount vendor instead of a trusted advisor.

My wake-up call came during a project for a regional bank. They needed someone to upgrade their loan processing system, and I bid $15,000 for work that should have been priced at $25,000. I got the project, but the client constantly questioned my recommendations and second-guessed my decisions. They treated me like hired help, not like an expert.

Halfway through the project, they brought in another consultant to "review" my work. This guy charged $200 an hour compared to my

$75, and they hung on his every word. He rubber-stamped everything I'd done, collected $3,000 for two days of work, and walked away. Meanwhile, I was grinding through six weeks of implementation for less money than he made in a week.

That's when I realized pricing isn't just about covering your costs and making a profit. It's about positioning yourself in the market and managing client expectations.

Here's how I price projects now. First, I figure out what the project is worth to the client, not what it costs me to deliver. If I'm saving them $100,000 a year in operational costs, my fee should reflect that value. If I'm helping them enter a new market worth millions, I should get paid accordingly.

Second, I research what other consultants charge for similar work. I don't want to be the cheapest option, but I also can't be so expensive that I price myself out of realistic consideration. I aim for the upper third of the market range.

Third, I factor in the pain-in-the-ass coefficient. Some clients are easy to work with and some make you want to drink heavily. Difficult clients get charged more because dealing with them takes extra time and energy. Life's too short to work with jerks for discount rates.

I learned about difficult clients during a project for a software company run by a micromanaging CEO. This guy wanted daily updates, questioned every decision, and changed his mind constantly. A project that should have taken four weeks stretched to eight weeks because of his constant interference. I made barely any money on that project, but I learned to spot the warning signs and price accordingly.

Now when I sense a client might be difficult, I add 25% to my normal rate. If they balk at the price, I'm happy to walk away. If they accept it, at least I'm getting paid fairly for the aggravation.

For project pricing, I prefer fixed bids over hourly rates whenever possible. Fixed bids force me to think carefully about scope and timeline, and they give clients predictable costs. But fixed bids only work if you have a detailed SOW and solid change control process.

The key to successful fixed-bid pricing is padding your estimates appropriately. I add 20% to my best-case scenario to cover unexpected complications. If everything goes perfectly, I make a nice profit. If problems arise, I've got buffer built in.

One practical use for AI: market rate research. Describe your project type and ask what consultants typically charge for similar work. It won't give you a definitive number, but it'll give you a range to pressure-test your instincts against, and it can surface considerations you hadn't thought of — regulatory compliance overhead, specialized tooling costs, industry-specific risk factors. Use it the way you'd use a knowledgeable colleague: as a starting point for thinking, not as the final word.

When I do charge hourly rates, I quote project ranges instead of open-ended hourly billing. Something like: "This project will require 40-60 hours at $150 per hour, for a total cost of $6,000-$9,000." This gives the client budget predictability while protecting me if the scope expands.

Your contract protects you when things go wrong, and things will go wrong. I've had clients refuse to pay, demand free work beyond the agreed scope, and try to hold me liable for problems I didn't create. A good contract prevents most of these issues.

Your contract should nail down payment terms clearly. I require 50% upfront for new clients and net-15 payment terms for the balance. The upfront payment covers my initial costs and demonstrates the client's commitment. The net-15 terms keep cash flow moving.

I learned about payment terms the hard way during a project for a struggling retail chain. They hired me to implement a new point-of-sale system, and I foolishly agreed to net-60 payment terms. By the time I finished the project, they were three months behind on payments to all their vendors. I eventually got paid, but only after six months of collection efforts.

Your contract should also limit your liability. Consulting work carries inherent risks, and you can't be responsible for every possible outcome. My contracts cover language like: "Consultant's total liability shall not exceed the total amount paid under this agreement."

Cover a termination clause that protects both parties. Either side should be able to end the contract with reasonable notice, and you should get paid for work completed up to the termination date.

Make sure your contract addresses intellectual property ownership. Generally, the client owns the work product they're paying for, but you should retain ownership of your methods, tools, and general knowledge.

Finally, cover a dispute resolution clause. Any disagreements get handled through mediation or arbitration instead of expensive litigation. This saves both parties time and money if problems arise.

One question nobody answers directly: what do you charge when you're just starting out and have no baseline? The honest answer is that you research and then commit. Look up what consultants in your field charge on platforms like Upwork or LinkedIn, call a few staffing agencies and ask what they bill for your skillset, and talk to anyone you know who consults independently. Then take the midpoint of what you find and add 20%. Most new consultants underestimate their market value because they're comparing themselves to employees rather than to other consultants. Your rate should reflect the fact that you carry your own overhead, pay your own taxes, provide no benefits to the client, and disappear when the work is done. That's worth something.

The goal of good pricing and contracts isn't to maximize what you extract from each client. It's to create fair, sustainable relationships that lead to repeat business and referrals. Price yourself appropriately, protect yourself legally, and deliver exceptional value. Do that consistently, and you'll build a consulting practice that supports the lifestyle you want.

Pricing models and payment arrangements

How you price your work and when you get paid determines whether consulting becomes a profitable business or an expensive hobby. Most consultants focus on hourly rates while ignoring the pricing model and payment timing that drive profitability.

I learned this lesson during my first year of consulting when I had plenty of work but was constantly broke. I was charging competitive hourly rates and landing good projects, but my cash flow was a disaster. Clients paid me 30-60 days after I submitted invoices, meaning I was providing free financing for their projects.

The breaking point came during a four-month project for a manufacturing company. I was working full-time on their inventory system upgrade, billing $125 per hour, and generating $20,000 per month in invoices. On paper, I was doing great. In reality, I was living on credit cards because the client paid invoices 45 days late.

Three months into the project, I had $60,000 in outstanding receivables and $200 in my checking account. I couldn't make my mortgage payment and had to borrow money from my father to buy groceries. That's when I realized that hourly billing with delayed payment was a recipe for financial stress.

Now I structure every engagement to ensure positive cash flow from day one. I get paid before I work, not after. This fundamental shift transformed my consulting practice from a cash flow nightmare into a sustainable business.

There are three basic pricing models for consulting work: fixed bid, hourly billing, and retainer arrangements. Each has advantages and disadvantages, but the key is matching the pricing model to the project type and managing payment timing to protect your cash flow.

Fixed bid pricing works well for projects with clearly defined scope and deliverables. The client knows exactly what they're getting and what it will cost. You know exactly what you need to deliver and how much you'll make. Both parties can plan accordingly.

I use fixed bid pricing for technical implementations where the requirements are well understood and the work is straightforward. Database migrations, system integrations, and software installations all lend themselves to fixed pricing because the scope is clear and the deliverables are measurable.

The key to successful fixed bid pricing is detailed scope definition and change control. Your statement of work must spell out exactly what's included and what's not. Any changes to scope get handled through formal change orders with additional charges.

I add 20-30% to my time estimates for fixed bid projects to account for scope creep and unexpected complications. If everything goes perfectly, I make a nice profit. If problems arise, I've got buffer built in to handle them.

Fixed bid pricing also allows you to capture the value of efficiency improvements. If you find ways to complete the work faster than estimated, the time savings go directly to your profit margin. This creates incentives to work efficiently and invest in better tools and processes.

Hourly billing works better for projects with undefined scope or where the client wants flexibility to adjust requirements as the work progresses. Strategic consulting, troubleshooting, and crisis recovery situations often require hourly billing because you can't predict how much time will be needed.

The challenge with hourly billing is managing client expectations and your own cash flow. Clients worry about unlimited costs, and you worry about getting paid for work already completed. Both concerns can be addressed through proper structuring.

I bill hourly work in advance blocks of 10-20 hours. Before starting any hourly project, the client pays for the first block of time. When that time is consumed, they pay for the next block before I continue working. This ensures I always have payment in hand for work already completed.

For a $150 per hour project, I might require payment of $3,000 upfront for the first 20 hours of work. As I complete tasks, I track time against this prepayment. When I've used 15 hours, I invoice for the next 20-hour block and stop working until payment is received.

This approach protects my cash flow while giving clients predictable cost increments. They know that each payment covers an amount of work, and I know that I'll never have more than a few hours of unbilled time at risk.

Retainer arrangements work well for ongoing advisory relationships where the client wants regular access to your expertise but can't predict exactly when they'll need help. The client pays a monthly fee for a amount of your time, whether they use it or not.

I use retainer arrangements for clients who need ongoing database support, strategic advice, or technical guidance. They pay a flat monthly fee that covers up to a certain number of hours per month. If they use fewer hours, they don't get a refund. If they need more hours, they pay additional charges.

A retainer might be $5,000 per month for up to 20 hours of consulting time. The client gets priority access to my schedule and predictable monthly costs. I get guaranteed monthly revenue and a stable relationship with a valued client.

Retainer arrangements require clear boundaries about what's included and how time is tracked. My retainer covers phone consultations, email advice, and hands-on work, but excludes travel time or work requiring other specialists.

Payment timing is more important than pricing structure for maintaining healthy cash flow. I require payment before work begins on every project, regardless of the pricing model. This isn't negotiable, and clients who resist this requirement usually turn out to be payment problems later.

For fixed bid projects, I require 50% payment before starting and the remaining 50% at project completion. Large projects get broken into milestones with payments at each stage. I never begin work until the first payment clears my bank account.

For hourly projects, clients pay for time blocks in advance as described above. For retainer arrangements, clients pay monthly fees in advance on the first of each month.

This payment structure eliminates most collection problems because clients are paying for future work instead of work already completed. If they don't pay, I simply stop working. There's no chasing unpaid invoices or wondering if I'll get paid for work already delivered.

Some clients resist paying in advance, especially large corporations with bureaucratic purchasing processes. I explain that advance payment is standard practice for professional services and protects both parties by ensuring clear financial commitment before work begins.

Organizations typically pay net 30 to net 90 and are often late even then. Large corporations have bureaucratic payment processes that can stretch invoices for months, regardless of the original payment terms. I've had Fortune 500 companies take 120 days to pay 30-day invoices without any consequences.

People understand that freelancers need the income and usually pay fast, within a week of receiving an invoice. They're spending their own money and feel the urgency of payment in a way that corporate purchasing departments don't.

If you work primarily with organizations, you'll generally need to start work before receiving full payment. The key is minimizing your exposure by requiring big down payments and breaking large projects into smaller milestones. A 50% down payment on a corporate project protects you better than trying to collect the full amount after delivery.

If clients cannot pay in advance due to internal policies, I require payment terms of net-10 days maximum with late payment penalties. But I prefer to walk away from clients who won't pay upfront instead of creating cash flow problems for my business.

Down payments serve multiple purposes beyond cash flow protection. They demonstrate client commitment to the project and filter out tire-kickers who aren't serious about moving forward. Clients who are willing to pay upfront are generally more engaged and easier to work with.

I've found that projects with advance payments have fewer scope changes, less client interference, and better outcomes than projects with traditional billing. When clients have money invested upfront, they're more motivated to make the project successful.

Milestone payments work well for large projects that span several months. Instead of waiting until the end for payment, I break the project into phases with payments at each milestone. This maintains cash flow while giving clients confidence that payments are tied to delivered results.

A six-month system implementation might have milestones for requirements analysis, design approval, development completion, testing, and go-live. Each milestone triggers a payment that covers the next phase of work.

Monthly billing can work for long-term engagements, but I still require advance payment for each month. Instead of invoicing at month-end and waiting for payment, clients pay at the beginning of each month for that month's work.

The key principle is simple: always receive payment before work. This protects your cash flow, demonstrates client commitment, and eliminates most collection problems. Consultants who provide financing for their clients are asking for financial trouble.

Client education is important when implementing advance payment requirements. Many clients are accustomed to traditional invoicing and may need explanation about why advance payment benefits both parties. I frame it as professional standard practice instead of a lack of trust.

Some clients will push back on advance payment requirements or ask for extended payment terms. These conversations reveal a lot about the client's financial stability and attitude toward professional services. Clients who respect your payment requirements are usually easier to work with in other areas as well.

Contract language should clearly nail down payment terms, covering amounts, timing, and consequences for late payment. I include clauses that allow me to stop work immediately if payments are late and resume charging interest on overdue amounts.

The goal isn't to be difficult or inflexible about payment terms. It's to create sustainable business practices that allow you to focus on delivering excellent work instead of worrying about cash flow and collections.

One thing nobody warns independent consultants about: the financial infrastructure of going solo is more expensive than people expect. Health insurance is the big one. If you left an employer who covered your premiums, you're about to find out what insurance actually costs. Budget for it before you price your first project — not after. The same applies to self-employment tax (you pay both halves of Social Security and Medicare, roughly 15% on top of income tax), quarterly estimated tax payments, and retirement savings you now fund entirely yourself. None of this is complicated, but it all needs to be factored into your rate before you quote anything. A consultant charging $100 per hour who hasn't accounted for these costs is often netting less than a $60-per-hour employee. Get an accountant who works with independent contractors in your first year. It will save you more than it costs.

If you're doing good work and still broke, look at when you get paid. Payment timing isn't a detail. It's the difference between a consulting business and an expensive hobby.

| 5 |

Never work for free

Working for free is the fastest way to destroy your consulting practice. Free work devalues your expertise, attracts the wrong clients, and wastes time you could spend on activities that generate revenue. The only exception to this rule is school internships, where the educational value justifies the investment.

Most consultants fall into the free work trap because they think it will lead to paid opportunities. Potential clients promise future projects, referrals, or long-term relationships in exchange for free consulting. These promises almost never materialize, and you end up doing real work for imaginary compensation.

I learned about free work the expensive way during my second year of consulting. A local nonprofit organization contacted me about upgrading their donor management system. They explained that their budget was extremely limited, but they had connections with several wealthy board members who might need consulting services for their businesses.

The nonprofit director painted a compelling picture of future opportunities. She claimed that one board member owned a chain of retail stores, another ran a manufacturing company, and a third was a venture capitalist who funded tech startups. If I could help them with their database project, she was sure they would recommend me for lucrative paid work.

I spent three weeks analyzing their existing system, designing a new database structure, and implementing the migration. The work was complex because their data was messy and their requirements kept changing. I treated it like a paid project, delivering the same quality I would provide to any client.

The project was successful. The new system worked well, and the nonprofit was thrilled with the results. They sent a nice thank-you letter praising my expertise and professionalism. But none of the promised referrals materialized. The board members never contacted me, and the nonprofit never hired me for additional work.

That three weeks of free work could have been spent marketing to paying clients, improving my skills, or developing new service offerings. Instead, I gave away valuable expertise and got nothing in return except a warm feeling about helping a good cause.

The fundamental problem with free work is that it attracts people who don't value consulting services. Clients who expect free work rarely become clients who pay market rates. They're looking for cheap solutions, not professional expertise, and they'll continue seeking free alternatives instead of paying for quality.

Free work also sets terrible precedents for ongoing relationships. If you start working for free, clients assume that's your normal rate. When you try to transition to paid work, they feel like you're suddenly charging them for something that used to be free. The relationship dynamic is fundamentally damaged.

I've seen consultants get trapped in cycles of free work where clients keep promising payment for the "next" project while asking for more free consulting on the current one. These situations drag on for months while consultants hope that eventually the client will start paying. They almost never do.

The time you spend on free work has enormous opportunity cost. Those hours could be used for marketing activities that generate paying clients, educational activities that improve your skills, or business development that expands your service offerings. All of these alternatives are better investments than working for free.

Marketing activities like content creation, networking events, and prospect outreach have measurable returns when done consistently. An hour spent writing a technical blog post or attending a professional meetup is more likely to generate future revenue than an hour of free consulting work.

Educational activities like online courses, certification programs, or skill development workshops improve your expertise and allow you to charge higher rates. Time invested in learning new technologies or methodologies increases your market value and opens up new service opportunities.

Business development activities like proposal writing, partnership discussions, or service packaging create systematic approaches to generating revenue. These investments pay dividends across multiple clients instead of benefiting just one organization that doesn't want to pay.

Some consultants justify free work as "marketing expense" or "relationship building," but this rationalization ignores better alternatives for achieving the same goals. If you want to demonstrate your expertise, create case studies from paid projects. If you want to build relationships, attend industry events where you can meet multiple prospects simultaneously.

The "exposure" argument for free work is ridiculous in consulting. Consulting is a relationship-based business where referrals come from satisfied clients who paid for your services. Free work doesn't create the same level of commitment and satisfaction as paid engagements, so it rarely leads to strong referrals.

Portfolio building is another common justification for free work, but it's usually unnecessary for experienced consultants and counterproductive for beginners. Experienced consultants should have plenty of paid work to showcase. Beginning consultants are better off starting with small, low-priced projects that at least cover their costs.

Charitable work deserves consideration because many consultants want to support causes they care about. If you want to help nonprofits or community organizations, budget time and money for charitable contributions instead of treating consulting work as charity. Set clear boundaries about how much pro bono work you'll do each year and stick to those limits.

When I do pro bono work now, I treat it as a business expense with clear limits and expectations. I budget 20 hours per year for charitable consulting and choose projects that align with causes I care about. The work is still professional quality, but I don't expect it to generate revenue or referrals.

The "foot in the door" strategy rarely works in consulting because it's based on a false premise about how clients make purchasing decisions. Clients don't hire consultants because they got free work previously. They hire consultants because they have problems that need solving and budget to pay for solutions.

Discounting your rates to win projects is different from working for free, but it creates similar problems. Clients who hire you based on low prices rarely become clients who pay premium rates later. They're price-sensitive buyers who will leave you for cheaper alternatives as soon as they find them.

I learned to distinguish between clients who value expertise and clients who only care about price. Value-focused clients ask about methodology, experience, and outcomes. Price-focused clients lead with budget constraints and comparisons to cheaper alternatives. The latter group rarely converts to profitable long-term relationships.

School internships are the only legitimate exception to the no-free-work rule because they provide educational value that justifies the investment. Internships offer learning opportunities, mentorship, and professional network building that can be valuable for early career development.

But even internship programs should have clear educational components and time limits. Unpaid internships that consist of routine work without learning opportunities are just free labor, not educational experiences. Make sure any internship provides genuine skill development and industry exposure.

Some clients try to disguise requests for free work as "trials," "tests," or "proof of concept" projects. These requests are usually attempts to get free consulting under the pretense of evaluating your capabilities. Legitimate client evaluations can be handled through references, portfolio reviews, and detailed proposals.

If clients want to see examples of your work, provide case studies from previous projects. If they want to understand your methodology, explain your approach during the sales process. If they want to evaluate your technical skills, discuss your experience and certifications. None of these evaluation methods require free work.

Spec work, where multiple consultants compete by providing free solutions to the same problem, is problematic because it encourages clients to expect free consulting as part of the sales process. These competitions usually go to the cheapest bidder instead of the best solution, making them poor investments of time.

I recently heard about a clever version of this scam from the ghostwriting world. Someone was looking for a ghostwriter for a book project and asked potential writers to submit a "sample chapter" picked randomly from the outline. They claimed this would help them evaluate writing style and expertise.

What they were doing was asking a couple dozen ghostwriters to each write a different chapter of their book for free. Each writer thought they were competing for the project by writing one sample chapter. In reality, the "client" was assembling an entire book from free chapters written by different people. Not one of the ghostwriters fell for the scam - they all recognized it for what it was and declined.

I decline all spec work requests and explain that I don't compete on free solutions. Instead, I offer to discuss the project requirements and provide a detailed proposal that outlines my approach and methodology. Clients who are serious about hiring consultants are willing to evaluate proposals instead of demanding free work.

The scarcity mindset drives many free work decisions. Consultants worry that turning down free opportunities will hurt their chances of finding paid work. This thinking is backwards because free work reduces your availability for paying clients and creates a reputation as someone who works cheaply.

Abundance mindset recognizes that there are plenty of clients willing to pay for professional expertise. Your job is to find those clients instead of trying to convert non-paying prospects into paying clients. Focus your time and energy on marketing to people who have budgets and understand the value of consulting services.

Some consultants offer free initial consultations as part of their sales process. This can work if the consultations are brief, focused on understanding requirements, and designed to demonstrate expertise. But beware of "consultations" that turn into extensive analysis or problem-solving sessions.

I offer free 30-minute discovery calls to qualified prospects. These calls focus on understanding their situation and explaining how I might help. I don't provide solutions or detailed analysis during these calls. If prospects want more extensive consultation, that becomes a paid engagement.

Never work for free. Your time and expertise have value, and giving them away for free trains the market to expect consulting services without compensation. Invest your unpaid time in marketing, education, and business development activities that generate long-term returns instead of one-time benefits for clients who don't want to pay.

The only clients worth having are clients who understand the value of professional expertise and have budgets to pay for it. Everything else is a distraction from building a profitable consulting practice.

| 6 |

Red flags

Some clients will destroy your business if you let them. Learning to spot warning signs early can save you from projects that turn into nightmares, relationships that damage your reputation, and payment problems that threaten your financial stability.

I used to think that any client willing to pay my rates was a good client. This naive approach led me into several disasters that taught me the hard way that some business isn't worth having. Now I screen potential clients as carefully as they screen me, and I walk away from projects that show too many red flags.

The biggest red flag is clients who want to start work immediately without proper planning or contracts. These clients create artificial urgency to pressure you into beginning work before you've thought through the risks or negotiated proper terms.

I once had a potential client call me on a Friday afternoon claiming they needed a database migration completed by Monday morning. Their "critical system" was failing, and they were desperate for help. The urgency felt real, and the project seemed straightforward, so I agreed to start work over the weekend.

By Sunday evening, I realized the project was far more complex than originally described. The client had multiple databases that needed migration, not just one. The data was corrupted and required extensive cleanup. The target system wasn't properly configured.

What should have been a four-hour migration turned into a 30-hour nightmare.

When I submitted my invoice for the weekend work, the client disputed the charges. They claimed I had quoted a fixed price for the entire project, which wasn't true. They refused to pay for the extra time needed to handle problems they hadn't disclosed upfront.

The artificial urgency had been a tactic to get me to start work without a proper contract or scope definition. I spent more time fighting about payment than I did on the technical work, and I never got fully paid for the weekend I sacrificed.

Now I never start work without a signed contract and clear scope definition, regardless of how urgent the client claims the situation is. Real emergencies are rare, and clients who can't wait for proper planning usually have other problems that will surface later.

Clients who negotiate aggressively on price are usually trouble throughout the entire engagement. They see consulting services as a commodity and will try to squeeze you on every aspect of the project, not just the initial fee.

Price-focused clients demand the lowest possible rates, the fastest possible delivery, and the broadest possible scope. They want champagne results at beer prices and get angry when reality doesn't match their unrealistic expectations.

I've learned to avoid clients who open negotiations by asking for discounts, comparing my rates to cheaper alternatives, or trying to bundle multiple projects together for volume pricing. These clients will nickel-and-dime you throughout the project and complain about every invoice.

Clients who refuse to provide references from previous consultants are hiding something. Good clients are happy to connect you with other professionals they've worked with. Bad clients make excuses about confidentiality or claim they've never used consultants before.

When clients do provide references, pay attention to the types of projects and the outcomes. If all their previous consultants worked on small, short-term projects, they might have trouble maintaining long-term professional relationships. If references mention communication problems or scope changes, those issues will probably affect your project too.

I always call at least two references for big projects. I ask about payment history, communication style, scope management, and overall satisfaction. References who seem hesitant to give strong recommendations are telling you something important.

Clients who can't clearly explain their problem or desired outcome will waste enormous amounts of your time on scope clarification and requirements gathering. They know something is wrong but haven't done the basic thinking needed to articulate what they want fixed.

These clients often use phrases like "we need to modernize our systems" or "our processes are inefficient" without providing details about current problems or success criteria. They expect you to figure out what they need, creating unlimited scope for requirements analysis.

I've learned to push back during initial conversations when clients can't provide clear problem statements. If they can't explain what's broken or what success looks like, they're not ready to hire a consultant. The discovery process should clarify solutions, not define the basic problem.

Clients who insist on managing every detail of your work don't understand the value of professional expertise. They want to dictate the tools you use, the methodologies you follow, and the order in which you complete tasks.

Micromanaging clients often have control issues that extend beyond the technical work. They want frequent status updates, detailed time reports, and approval authority over minor decisions. Working with these clients feels like being an employee instead of an independent consultant.

I explain during the sales process that I expect autonomy in how I deliver the agreed-upon results. Clients who resist this expectation usually want cheap labor instead of professional expertise.

Payment red flags cover requests for extended payment terms, resistance to advance payments, and complex approval processes for invoices. Clients with cash flow problems will create cash flow problems for you.

Be especially wary of clients who want to tie payments to subjective milestones like "client satisfaction" or "successful implementation." These payment terms give clients unlimited leverage to withhold payment if they're unhappy with any aspect of the project.

I've also learned to avoid clients who want to pay with equity, revenue sharing, or other non-cash arrangements. These payment structures might work for long-term partnerships, but they're inappropriate for most consulting projects.

Scope creep warnings start with clients who describe projects as "simple" or "straightforward" when they're clearly complex. They often underestimate the complexity of their own systems and processes, leading to unrealistic expectations about timeline and cost.

Clients who frequently use phrases like "while you're at it" or "one small addition" during initial conversations will expand scope throughout the project. They see additional requests as minor favors instead of billable work.

Communication red flags start with clients who are slow to respond to questions, frequently reschedule meetings, or delegate important decisions to people who aren't available. Poor communication during the sales process predicts poor communication during the project.

Clients who communicate primarily through intermediaries or constantly change the primary contact person create confusion and delays. You need direct access to decision-makers to deliver results efficiently.

Technology red flags cover clients with severely outdated systems, no IT support, or unrealistic expectations about what technology can accomplish. These clients often want modern solutions but aren't willing to make the infrastructure investments needed to support them.

Be especially careful with clients who want to integrate with systems they can't adequately describe or provide access to. Hidden technical complexity will destroy your timeline and budget estimates.

The key to avoiding problem clients is trusting your instincts when red flags appear. If something feels wrong during the initial conversations, it probably is. No project is worth the stress and financial risk of working with truly difficult clients.

I've walked away from projects worth tens of thousands of dollars because the clients showed too many warning signs. In every case, I later learned that other consultants had similar problems with those same clients.

A sustainable consulting practice means being selective about the clients you accept. Focus on developing relationships with clients who value professional expertise, communicate clearly, pay promptly, and treat consultants as partners instead of vendors.

Red flags are your early warning system for avoiding disasters. Pay attention to them, and you'll save yourself enormous amounts of stress, frustration, and financial loss.

| 7 |

Reading your client

Chapter 6 was about screening clients before you take them. This chapter is about what to do once you have them. Because some clients pass the red flag test and still turn out to be difficult — and knowing which type you're dealing with early makes the difference between a managed project and a slow disaster.

Every client has a personality, and if you can't read it quickly, you're going to have problems. Some clients micromanage every detail. Others disappear for weeks and expect you to read their minds. Some make decisions fast. Others form committees to decide what color pens to order.

Learning to read clients early in the relationship will save you countless headaches and help you manage projects more effectively. Miss the signals, and you'll find yourself constantly frustrated and fighting uphill battles you could have avoided.

I learned this lesson during a project for a manufacturing company that made specialized industrial equipment. The initial meeting went great. The CEO, a guy named Brantley, seemed decisive and knowledgeable. He explained exactly what he wanted: a new inventory management system to replace their outdated paper-based tracking.

Brantley approved my proposal within two days and wanted to start immediately. I thought I'd landed the perfect client. Boy, was I wrong.

Three days into the project, Brantley called to "check in" on my progress. Then he called again the next day. And the day after that. By the end of the first week, he was calling twice a day and dropping by my temporary office to look over my shoulder.

He questioned every design decision, wanted to approve every screen layout, and insisted on reviewing every line of code before I could move to the next task. A project that should have taken six weeks stretched to four months because of his constant interference.

I should have seen it coming. During our initial meeting, Brantley mentioned that he'd fired the last three consultants because they "didn't understand his vision." He talked about being personally involved in every aspect of his business, down to approving vacation requests for hourly workers. All the warning signs were there, but I was so focused on closing the deal that I ignored them.

Now I pay attention to these signals from the first conversation. Micromanagers reveal themselves quickly if you know what to look for. They use phrases like "I like to stay involved" and "I want to make sure we're on the right track." They ask detailed questions about your process and want to know exactly how you plan to approach each task.

There's nothing wrong with micromanagers if you plan for them. Build extra communication time into your schedule. Send daily status updates even when nothing has changed. Schedule regular check-in meetings so they don't feel the need to interrupt you constantly. Price the project to account for the extra hand-holding time.

On the other end of the spectrum are the hands-off clients. These people hire you and then vanish. They assume you'll figure everything out on your own and deliver exactly what they want without any guidance or feedback.

I ran into this type during a project for a real estate development company. The owner, Patricia, hired me to build a project management system for tracking construction timelines and budgets. Our kickoff meeting lasted 20 minutes. She gave me a brief overview of what she wanted and told me to "make it happen."

For the next month, I sent weekly status reports and received no response. I emailed questions about requirements and got radio silence. When I called her office, her assistant said she was "in meetings" or "out of town."

Halfway through the project, I realized I was building the wrong thing. Patricia finally responded to one of my emails, and it became clear that her vision for the system was completely different from what I was developing. We had to scrap three weeks of work and start over.

Hands-off clients aren't bad, but they require a different approach. You need to pin them down for detailed requirements discussions upfront. Get everything in writing and force them to approve major decisions before you proceed. Build review points into your timeline and don't continue until you get their sign-off.

Then there are the committee clients. These organizations can't make decisions without involving half the company. Every choice gets debated, analyzed, and studied to death.

I experienced this during a project for a mid-sized insurance company. They wanted a new claims processing system, and the project team included representatives from IT, operations, customer service, accounting, and legal. Getting approval for anything required a meeting with all six departments.

Changing a button label on a screen required a two-hour discussion about user experience, regulatory compliance, and brand consistency. Adding a new report required three meetings to debate the format, content, and distribution list. A project that should have taken two months took eight months because every decision went through committee hell.

Committee clients aren't inherently evil, but they'll kill your timeline if you don't manage them properly. Identify the real decision-maker early and build a relationship with that person. Schedule group meetings for major milestones, but handle day-to-day decisions through smaller groups or individual conversations.

The most dangerous clients are the ones who can't tell you what they want but insist they'll know it when they see it. These people hire you to solve a problem they can't articulate and expect you to read their minds.

I remember a project for a consulting firm that wanted to "modernize their image" with a new website. The managing partner, Douglas, couldn't explain what "modern" meant but rejected every design I showed him. After six rounds of revisions, I finally asked him to show me websites he liked. He couldn't name a single one.

We went around in circles for weeks. Douglas would say things like "make it more professional" or "add some pizzazz" without explaining what those terms meant. I eventually completed the project, but it took twice as long as it should have and left both of us frustrated.

These clients require extreme patience and a structured discovery process. You have to drag requirements out of them through detailed questioning and iterative prototyping. Show them lots of examples and force them to explain what they like and don't like about each one.

The best clients are the ones who know what they want, communicate clearly, make decisions quickly, and trust you to do your job. They're involved enough to provide guidance but don't micromanage your work. They respond to emails promptly and give you the information you need to succeed.

I've been lucky to work with many clients like this over the years. These relationships are profitable, enjoyable, and often lead to additional work. When you find clients like this, take excellent care of them and do everything possible to exceed their expectations.

Learning to read clients takes practice, but the investment pays off quickly. Pay attention to how they communicate during the sales process. Notice how they make decisions and what level of detail they want. Ask about their experience with previous consultants and what went well or poorly.

Trust your instincts. If something feels off during the initial conversations, it probably is. A bad client relationship will make your life miserable no matter how much money is involved. Sometimes the best decision is to walk away before you sign the contract.

| 8 |

Controlling change

Change will kill your project faster than a bad client, unrealistic deadlines, or incompetent team members. Every consulting project experiences change. The question isn't whether change will happen, but how you'll handle it when it does.

I've seen perfectly good projects turn into disasters because consultants couldn't say no to "small" changes. I've also seen consultants lose clients because they were too rigid about modifications that made perfect business sense. The key is controlling change, not preventing it.

My first real lesson in change control came during a project for a retail chain that sold outdoor gear. They hired me to build a new point-of-sale system for their 12 stores. The original scope was straightforward: basic inventory tracking, sales reporting, and integration with their existing accounting software.

Two weeks into the project, the owner called me with an idea. A competitor had just launched a customer loyalty program, and he wanted to add similar functionality to our system. "It's just a simple database," he said. "Shouldn't take more than a day or two."

I was young and eager to please, so I agreed. Adding customer tracking didn't seem like a big deal. Famous last words.

That "simple" loyalty program triggered an avalanche of additional changes. They wanted email marketing integration to communicate with loyalty members. Then they wanted different discount rules for different customer tiers. Then they wanted to track purchasing patterns to identify their best customers.

By the time I delivered the final system, it included inventory management, sales reporting, accounting integration, customer loyalty tracking, email marketing, promotional pricing, purchase history analysis, and automated reorder alerts. The project took four months instead of six weeks and cost them three times the original budget.

The worst part? The client was angry about the overruns even though he'd requested every single change. In his mind, these were all "minor additions" that shouldn't have affected the timeline or budget.

That's when I learned that clients have no idea how changes affect project complexity. What seems like a small modification to them often requires major architectural changes behind the scenes. Your job is to educate them about these impacts and manage the change process professionally.

Now I handle change requests very differently. First, I acknowledge that the request makes business sense. I don't want clients to think I'm being difficult or trying to pad the bill. I explain that I understand why they want the change and agree it would be valuable.

Then I explain exactly what the change involves. I break down the technical requirements, identify any dependencies, and estimate the time needed for design, development, testing, and implementation. I make sure they understand that change often affects more than just the obvious areas.

Using that loyalty program example, I would have explained that adding customer tracking required database schema changes, new user interface screens, integration with the payment processing module, modifications to the reporting system, and updates to the backup and security procedures. Each of these areas needed design time, development time, and testing time.

Next, I provide options for implementing the change. Sometimes the change can be added to the current project with minimal impact. Sometimes it makes more sense to complete the original scope and handle the change as a separate phase. Sometimes the change is so big that we need to rethink the entire project approach.

I always present at least two options: add it to the current project with clear time and cost impacts, or defer it to a future phase. This gives the client control over the decision while making the tradeoffs clear.

The key is documenting everything. Every change request gets written down with a detailed description, impact analysis, and cost estimate. The client must approve the change in writing before I start any additional work. No exceptions.

I learned about documentation the hard way during a project for a law firm. The managing partner kept asking for "quick changes" during our weekly status meetings. Add a field here, modify a report there, change the color scheme to match their new branding. Each change seemed trivial, so I just made the adjustments without formal documentation.

Three months later, when I submitted my final invoice, the managing partner disputed half the charges. He claimed he'd only authorized the original scope and demanded detailed justification for every hour beyond the initial estimate. I had notes about the changes but no formal approval documentation. It took six months and legal threats to collect payment.

Now every change gets documented with a formal change order that covers the description of the work, the time required, the cost impact, and the effect on the project timeline. Both parties sign the change order before any work begins.

Some clients resist this level of formality, especially for changes they consider minor. I explain that documentation protects both of us. It ensures we both understand exactly what work is being done and prevents misunderstandings later. I also point out that undocumented changes are the primary cause of project disputes and cost overruns.

Not all change requests should be approved. Sometimes clients ask for modifications that don't align with their business objectives or would compromise the project's success. Your job is to provide honest advice about these requests, even if it means pushing back on the client.

I remember a project for a manufacturing company where the CEO wanted to add real-time production monitoring to their inventory system. The functionality made sense, but implementing it required expensive hardware upgrades and additional software licenses that doubled the project cost.

Instead of just accepting the request, I proposed a phased approach. We completed the basic inventory system first, then evaluated the production monitoring requirements as a separate project. This allowed them to see immediate value from the original system and make a more informed decision about the additional investment.

The CEO appreciated my honesty and business perspective. We completed the inventory project on time and budget, and they hired me six months later to implement the production monitoring system after they'd secured additional funding.

Change control isn't about being inflexible or gouging clients for extra fees. It's about managing scope creep professionally and maintaining project quality. Uncontrolled change leads to budget overruns, missed deadlines, and frustrated clients. Proper change control leads to successful projects and satisfied customers.

The best change control process feels collaborative instead of bureaucratic. You want clients to feel comfortable suggesting improvements while understanding the impact of their requests. When you handle change professionally, clients trust your judgment and rely on your expertise to guide their decisions.

Change control isn't bureaucracy. It's the paper trail that proves the client asked for what they got, and the reason you get paid for it.

| 9 |

Controlling chaos

Chaos is the natural state of any project involving more than one person. Add tight deadlines, changing requirements, and competing priorities, and you've got a recipe for complete disaster. Your job as a consultant is to impose order on this chaos without becoming a dictator.

I learned about chaos management during one of my most challenging projects: implementing a new financial reporting system for a regional hospital network. The project involved five hospitals, three different accounting systems, dozens of department heads who all had opinions, and a board of directors breathing down everyone's necks.

The project started badly and got worse. The IT director at the main hospital insisted on using a different database platform than the one in our SOW. Two of the satellite hospitals were running on ancient systems that couldn't communicate with anything built after 1995. The CFO changed the reporting requirements every week based on feedback from various department heads.

Three weeks into what should have been a 12-week project, I was drowning. Team members were working on conflicting requirements. Nobody knew what the current specifications were. The client was frustrated because they weren't seeing progress. I was putting in 16-hour days and getting nowhere.

That's when I realized that working harder wasn't going to solve the problem. I needed to step back and impose some structure on the chaos.

The first step was getting everyone on the same page about what we were building. I called a meeting with all the key stakeholders and walked through the original SOW line by line. We identified what had changed, what was still valid, and what needed clarification.

This took an entire day, but it was the best day I spent on the project. By the end of the meeting, we had a clear understanding of the scope, a realistic timeline, and agreement from all parties about the priorities.

Next, I established a communication hierarchy. Instead of trying to manage relationships with 20 different people, I identified three key contacts: the IT director for technical issues, the CFO for business requirements, and the project sponsor for major decisions. Everyone else had to route their requests through one of these three people.

This sounds harsh, but it's essential for maintaining sanity. When anyone can interrupt you with questions, requests, or complaints, you'll spend all your time in meetings and none of your time working. A clear communication structure protects your time while ensuring that important issues get addressed.

I also implemented daily standup meetings with my core team. These 15-minute meetings covered what each person accomplished yesterday, what they planned to work on today, and any blockers they were facing. The meetings kept everyone aligned and allowed us to identify problems before they became disasters.

Some people think daily meetings are overkill, but they're wrong. When you're only meeting weekly, small problems have seven days to grow into big problems. Daily check-ins catch issues early when they're still easy to fix.

The key to effective standups is keeping them short and focused. No long discussions, no problem-solving sessions, no status reports. Just the facts: what you did, what you're doing, what's blocking you.

If issues need detailed discussion, schedule separate meetings with the right people.

Document everything, but don't drown in documentation. I keep a simple project log that tracks major decisions, changes, and issues. Nothing fancy, just a running record of what happened when. This proves invaluable when stakeholders forget what they agreed to or when you need to trace the source of a problem.

I also maintain an issues and decisions log. Every problem gets written down with a description, the impact, the proposed solution, and who's responsible for resolving it. This prevents issues from falling through the cracks and gives everyone visibility into what's being worked on.

AI has become useful here in a specific way: when a project is in chaos, it's often because the team has lost track of the current state. Dumping your project notes, email threads, and meeting summaries into an AI tool and asking it to produce a concise status summary can get everyone back on the same page faster than another two-hour meeting. It's not magic — you still have to review what it produces — but it compresses three hours of re-reading into fifteen minutes of editing.

The decisions log captures major choices and the reasoning behind them. Six months later, when someone questions why you chose approach A over approach B, you can point to the documented rationale instead of trying to remember what you were thinking.

Establish clear roles and responsibilities early in the project. Chaos often results from confusion about who's supposed to do what. Create a simple matrix that shows who's responsible for different types of decisions and activities.

The client might be responsible for defining business requirements while you're responsible for technical architecture. The client approves major design decisions while you handle day-to-day implementation choices. Having this clarity prevents the endless "I thought you were handling that" conversations.

Build buffers into your timeline for the unexpected. Murphy's Law applies to consulting projects in spades. Key team members will get sick at critical moments. Vendor deliveries will be late. Requirements will change at the last minute. Client systems will crash during testing.

I add 20% to my initial timeline estimates to account for these inevitable disruptions. If everything goes perfectly, I deliver early and look like a hero. If problems arise, I've got cushion built in to handle them without missing deadlines.

Sometimes chaos comes from external factors you can't control. During that hospital project, one of the satellite facilities got hit with a ransomware attack that took their entire network offline for three days. This completely disrupted our testing schedule and delayed the go-live date by two weeks.

When external factors cause problems, communicate the impact quickly and clearly. Don't try to absorb the delay or make up the lost time by cutting corners. Explain what happened, how it affects the project, and what options are available for getting back on track.

The client might choose to extend the timeline, reduce the scope, or add resources to make up lost time. But they need to make that choice with full understanding of the implications. Your job is to present the options clearly and implement whatever solution they choose.

Learn to recognize when chaos is spiraling out of control. Warning signs include team members working on conflicting tasks, requirements changing faster than you can implement them, and key stakeholders giving contradictory directions.

When you see these signs, stop everything and reset. Call a meeting with the key decision-makers and get alignment on priorities. Update your project plan to reflect the current reality. Communicate the new timeline and expectations to all stakeholders.

This feels like you're admitting failure, but you're taking control of the situation. Continuing to work without alignment just wastes time and money while frustrating everyone involved.

The goal isn't to eliminate chaos completely. That's impossible when you're dealing with people, technology, and changing business needs. The goal is to manage chaos well enough that it doesn't derail your project.

Good chaos management becomes second nature with practice. You'll develop instincts for spotting problems early, systems for maintaining alignment, and techniques for keeping projects moving forward despite the inevitable disruptions.

The consultant who can walk into a dumpster fire and come out with a working system is never short of work. That reputation is worth more than any resume line you'll ever write.

| 10 |

Communicating with the client

Client communication separates successful consultants from the ones who struggle to get repeat business. You can deliver brilliant technical work, but if you communicate poorly with the client, they'll remember the frustration more than the results.

Most consultants think communication means sending status reports and answering emails. That's part of it, but real communication is about building trust, managing expectations, and making the client feel confident about their investment in you.

I learned this lesson during a project for a manufacturing company that made custom furniture. The owner, a guy named Quinlan, hired me to build an inventory management system for their workshop. The technical requirements were straightforward, and I delivered exactly what he asked for on time and under budget.

The system worked perfectly. It tracked raw materials, managed work orders, and generated the reports Quinlan needed to run his business. By any objective measure, the project was a complete success.

But Quinlan was unhappy. During the final meeting, he complained that he never knew what was happening with the project. He said he felt like he was being kept in the dark and wasn't sure the money was being well spent. He paid the invoice but made it clear he wouldn't be hiring me again.

I was shocked. I'd been working my ass off to deliver a great system, and the client was unsatisfied because of communication issues I didn't even know existed.

That's when I realized that clients don't just buy technical solutions. They buy peace of mind. They want to feel confident that their project is in good hands and that their money is being spent wisely. Technical competence is table stakes. Communication is what separates you from the competition.

Now I start every project by establishing communication expectations with the client. How often do they want updates? What format works best for them? Do they prefer email, phone calls, or in-person meetings? What level of detail do they want?

Some clients want daily updates. Others prefer weekly summaries. Some want detailed technical information. Others just want to know if the project is on track. There's no universal right answer, but there is a wrong answer: assuming you know what the client wants without asking.

During the kickoff meeting, I have a conversation about communication preferences. I ask questions like: "How do you prefer to receive project updates? How much detail do you want in status reports? What's the best way to reach you if I have urgent questions? Who else needs to be kept informed about project progress?"

These seem like simple questions, but the answers vary dramatically from client to client. A busy CEO might want brief weekly emails with just the highlights. A hands-on project manager might want detailed daily reports with technical details. A committee-driven organization might need formal presentations for stakeholder groups.

Match your communication style to the client's preferences, not your own. If they like phone calls, call them. If they prefer email, send regular updates. If they want face-to-face meetings, schedule them. Your job is to make communication easy and comfortable for the client.

I also establish escalation procedures during the kickoff. What constitutes an urgent issue that requires immediate attention? Who should be contacted for different types of problems? How quickly do they expect responses to different types of requests?

This prevents misunderstandings when problems arise. If the client knows that system outages get escalated immediately but feature requests take 24 hours for a response, they won't panic when they don't hear back about a minor change request within an hour.

Regular status updates are the backbone of good client communication. Even when nothing dramatic is happening, clients want to know that work is progressing and their money is being spent productively.

I send weekly status reports that cover four things: what was accomplished this week, what's planned for next week, any issues or risks that need attention, and overall project status compared to the timeline and budget.

Keep status reports concise but informative. Clients are busy people who don't have time to read novels about your project. A one-page summary with clear headings and bullet points works better than a detailed narrative.

Focus on business impact instead of technical details. Don't say "Completed database schema design and implemented user authentication module." Say "Finished the foundation work that allows us to begin user interface development next week. The system will be ready for initial testing by month-end as planned."

Bad news doesn't improve with age. If you discover a problem that will affect the timeline, budget, or scope, tell the client immediately. Don't wait until your next scheduled update or hope that you'll find a way to fix it without their knowledge.

I learned this during a project for a law firm where a critical third-party integration turned out to be much more complex than expected. Instead of immediately informing the client, I spent two weeks trying to solve the problem myself. By the time I finally called them, what should have been a one-week delay had become a month-long setback.

The client was more upset about the communication delay than the technical problem. If I'd called them when I first discovered the issue, we could have explored alternatives or adjusted the timeline with minimal impact. My attempt to shield them from bad news just made things worse.

When delivering bad news, lead with the problem, explain the impact, and present solutions. Don't bury the bad news in a long explanation or try to soften it with unrelated good news. Be direct: "We've discovered a problem with the integration that will delay the go-live date by two weeks. Here are three options for addressing this issue."

Client questions deserve prompt, thoughtful responses. Even if you don't have a complete answer immediately, acknowledge the question and provide a timeline for a full response. Clients hate being ignored more than they hate waiting for answers.

I try to respond to client emails within four hours during business days, even if it's just to say "I received your message and will have a detailed response by tomorrow morning." This simple acknowledgment prevents clients from wondering if their message got lost or ignored.

When answering technical questions for non-technical clients, avoid jargon and explain things in business terms. Don't describe the technical architecture, explain how the solution will solve their business problem. Don't detail programming challenges, focus on what the client will be able to accomplish when the work is complete.

Use analogies and examples that relate to the client's business. If you're explaining database relationships to a retail client, compare it to how their inventory system tracks products and suppliers. If you're describing security measures to a healthcare client, relate it to patient privacy protections they already understand.

Document important decisions and agreements in writing. After phone conversations or meetings where big choices are made, send a follow-up email summarizing what was decided. This prevents misunderstandings later and gives both parties a record of what was agreed upon.

The follow-up doesn't need to be formal or lengthy. Something like: "Thanks for the productive call this morning. Just to confirm, we agreed to proceed with Option B for the reporting module, with delivery scheduled for the 15th. The additional cost will be $2,500 as discussed. Let me know if I misunderstood anything."

Proactive communication prevents most client relationship problems. Don't wait for clients to ask for updates, provide them regularly. Don't wait for them to express concerns, anticipate their needs and address issues before they become problems.

During one project for a restaurant chain, I noticed that the point-of-sale integration was taking longer than expected. Instead of waiting for the delay to affect the timeline, I called the client to explain the situation and proposed working overtime to stay on schedule. The client appreciated the heads-up and approved the overtime. What could have been a relationship-damaging delay became an opportunity to demonstrate commitment.

End-of-project communication is just as important as ongoing updates. Schedule a formal project wrap-up meeting to review what was accomplished, discuss any outstanding issues, and gather feedback about the process. This is your opportunity to reinforce the value you provided and set the stage for future work.

Ask for clear feedback about communication during the project. What worked well? What could have been improved? How did the communication compare to other consultants they've worked with? This information helps you refine your approach for future projects.

Great client communication isn't about being chatty or social. It's about being professional, reliable, and focused on the client's needs. When clients feel informed, confident, and valued, they become advocates for your work and sources of referrals for future business.

Clients forget the technical details fast. They remember how the project felt. If you want repeat business and referrals, make sure it felt good.

| 11 |

Meetings

Meetings will either make your consulting project a smooth success or turn it into a slow-motion disaster. There's no middle ground. Good meetings keep everyone aligned, resolve issues quickly, and move projects forward. Bad meetings waste time, create confusion, and generate more problems than they solve.

Most consultants are terrible at running meetings. They schedule too many, invite too many people, and let discussions wander all over the place. Then they wonder why their projects are constantly behind schedule and their clients are frustrated.

I learned about meeting management the hard way during a project for a regional insurance company. They wanted a new claims processing system, and the project involved representatives from six different departments. The IT director insisted on weekly status meetings with all stakeholders.

These meetings were supposed to last an hour. They regularly ran three hours or more. We'd start with a simple agenda item like "review database design" and somehow end up debating the company's vacation policy or discussing the parking situation at the corporate office.

Nobody prepared for the meetings. People would show up and ask basic questions about requirements we'd already agreed on. The same issues got discussed week after week with no resolution. Key decisions got postponed because the "right" person wasn't in the room.

After two months of this torture, I was ready to quit the project. The development work was going fine, but the meetings were consuming so much time that we were falling behind schedule. Worse, the constant rehashing of old decisions was confusing team members and making the client lose confidence in our progress.

That's when I decided to take control of the meeting process. I couldn't eliminate the meetings completely, but I could make them productive.

First, I started sending detailed agendas 24 hours before each meeting. Not just topic headings, but clear questions that needed answers and decisions that needed to be made. I included background information and relevant documents so people could prepare.

The agenda also included time allocations for each topic. This forced me to think realistically about what could be accomplished in the available time and gave participants a roadmap for the discussion.

Second, I established ground rules for participation. Side conversations were not allowed. Questions had to be relevant to the current topic. Anyone who hadn't read the agenda materials couldn't raise new issues during the meeting.

These rules sound harsh, but they transformed the meetings from social hour into working sessions. People started coming prepared because they knew they'd be called on to contribute.

Third, I took control of the discussion flow. When conversations started wandering, I'd redirect them back to the agenda. When people tried to revisit old decisions, I'd remind them that we'd already resolved those issues. When new topics came up, I'd add them to a parking lot for future discussion.

The key was being polite but firm about keeping things on track. I'd say something like "That's an interesting point, Marcus, but let's finish the current discussion first and come back to that later."

Fourth, I started ending meetings with clear action items and deadlines. Before anyone left the room, we'd review what had been decided, who was responsible for what, and when deliverables were due. I sent follow-up emails within 24 hours documenting these commitments.

This eliminated the confusion that plagued our early meetings. People knew exactly what they needed to do and when it needed to be done. More importantly, they knew that their commitments would be tracked and followed up on.

The transformation was dramatic. Our weekly meetings went from three-hour marathons to efficient one-hour sessions. We made more decisions, resolved more issues, and kept the project moving forward. The client started commenting on how well-organized and productive our meetings had become.

Not every meeting needs the same level of structure. Quick status updates can be handled informally. But any meeting that involves decision-making, problem-solving, or coordination between multiple people needs proper planning and management.

The most important rule about meetings is having a clear purpose. Don't schedule a meeting just because it's Thursday and you always meet on Thursday. Schedule meetings because there's something you need to accomplish that can't be handled through email or phone calls.

Meeting purposes fall into a few categories: information sharing, decision-making, problem-solving, and relationship building. Each type requires a different approach and structure.

Information sharing meetings are often the least necessary. Most information can be shared more efficiently through email, documents, or brief phone calls. Only schedule these meetings when you need interactive discussion or when the information is too complex for written communication.

Decision-making meetings require the most preparation. You need to present options clearly, provide relevant background information, and ensure that the right decision-makers are present. Come prepared with your recommendation and the reasoning behind it.

Problem-solving meetings work best with small groups of people who have relevant expertise. Large groups turn problem-solving into debating societies. Keep the attendance list tight and focused.

Relationship building meetings are often overlooked but critically important. These are the informal check-ins, project celebrations, and team-building sessions that keep everyone motivated and aligned. Don't underestimate their value just because they don't produce concrete deliverables.

Virtual meetings have become the norm for many consulting projects, especially when team members are distributed across different locations. The technology has improved dramatically, but virtual meetings still require different management techniques.

The biggest challenge with virtual meetings is maintaining engagement. It's much easier for people to multitask, check email, or tune out completely when they're sitting in their own office. You need to work harder to keep people involved and focused.

I use several techniques to improve virtual meeting engagement. First, I keep them shorter than in-person meetings. Attention spans are shorter when people are staring at screens. Second, I call on people by name more frequently to ensure they're paying attention. Third, I use screen sharing and visual aids to keep the discussion focused.

Virtual meetings also require better audio discipline. Background noise, echo, and poor connections can derail discussions quickly. I always use a headset and encourage others to do the same. I also establish protocols for muting and unmuting to minimize disruptions.

One-on-one meetings deserve attention because they're often the most productive meetings you'll have. These sessions allow for honest discussion without the political dynamics that affect group meetings.

I schedule regular one-on-ones with key client contacts and team members. These aren't status update sessions, they're relationship maintenance and issue identification meetings. People will tell you things privately that they'd never bring up in a group setting.

Meeting follow-up is just as important as the meeting itself. If decisions don't get documented and action items don't get tracked, the meeting was a waste of time. I send summary emails within 24 hours and follow up on commitments at the next meeting.

The summary doesn't need to be a verbatim transcript. Focus on decisions made, action items assigned, and any changes to project scope or timeline. Keep it concise but complete.

Learn to recognize when meetings are becoming counterproductive. Warning signs include the same issues being discussed repeatedly, key people missing sessions, or discussions that generate more questions than answers.

When meetings stop being useful, change the format, reduce the frequency, or eliminate them altogether. Don't keep having meetings just because they're on the calendar.

When you consistently run meetings that people find useful, they actually show up prepared. That alone will accelerate your projects more than any methodology.

| 12 |

Building and managing teams

Most consulting projects start as solo efforts, but sooner or later you'll need help. Maybe the project is too big for one person. Maybe you need skills you don't have. Maybe the client wants the work done faster than you can deliver alone. Whatever the reason, building and managing a team is one of the most challenging aspects of consulting.

I learned this lesson during a project for a manufacturing company that wanted to replace their entire enterprise resource planning system. The scope included inventory management, production scheduling, accounting integration, customer relationship management, and reporting across four facilities in different states.

I bid the project as a six-month effort for a team of five people. Sounded reasonable on paper. In reality, it was a nightmare.

The first problem was finding the right people. I needed a database architect, two application developers, a systems integration specialist, and someone who understood manufacturing operations. Three of these people had to be available to start within two weeks, and all of them had to work well together under pressure.

I started by calling everyone I knew. My network produced two solid candidates: Marcus, a database guy I'd worked with before, and Elena, an integration specialist from a previous project. Both were excellent at their jobs and available immediately.

Finding the other three people proved much harder. I posted jobs on freelancing websites and got hundreds of responses from people who clearly hadn't read the requirements. I interviewed dozens of candidates who looked good on paper but couldn't answer basic technical questions. I hired two developers who seemed competent during interviews but turned out to be disasters once the work started.

The first developer, Kevin, claimed five years of experience with our development platform. On his first day, it became obvious he'd never used the software before. He spent three days trying to connect to the database before admitting he didn't know what he was doing.

The second developer, Sarah, had solid technical skills but terrible communication habits. She would disappear for days without updating anyone on her progress. When problems arose, she'd work on them for weeks without asking for help or informing the team about delays.

By week six, I was behind schedule, over budget, and ready to fire half my team. That's when I realized I'd made fundamental mistakes in how I was building and managing the group.

First mistake: I hired people too quickly without properly vetting their skills. Technical interviews over the phone don't tell you much about someone's abilities. You need to see them work on real problems similar to what they'll face on your project.

Now I give all potential team members a small paid test project before hiring them for major work. Something that takes 4-8 hours and covers the core skills they'll need. This costs me a few hundred dollars upfront but saves thousands in the long run by weeding out people who can't do the work.

AI can help with the evaluation step. When a candidate submits test work, run it through an AI tool with a clear prompt: "Here is a code sample from a candidate for a database development role. What problems do you see? What questions would you ask?" You'll get a second opinion in two minutes that catches things you might gloss over when you're busy. It's not a replacement for reading the work yourself — the AI will miss context that only you have — but it's a useful check on your own blind spots, especially for skills adjacent to your core area.

Second mistake: I didn't establish clear communication expectations from the beginning. I assumed everyone would naturally keep the team informed about their progress and problems. Wrong assumption.

Now I require daily status updates from all team members. Nothing elaborate, just a quick email covering what they accomplished yesterday, what they're working on today, and any issues they're facing. Team members who don't communicate regularly don't stay on the team long.

Third mistake: I tried to manage everyone the same way. Different people need different levels of guidance and supervision. Marcus and Elena were experienced consultants who just needed clear requirements and occasional check-ins. Kevin needed intensive training and close supervision. Sarah needed structure and accountability.

You have to adapt your management style to each person's experience level and working style. Micromanaging experienced people will drive them away. Giving inexperienced people too much autonomy will lead to disaster.

The key is figuring out what each person needs quickly. Some people thrive with detailed specifications and regular feedback. Others prefer high-level direction and room to figure out the details themselves. Pay attention to how team members respond to different approaches and adjust accordingly.

A good team starts with a clear picture of exactly what skills you need. Don't just think about technical abilities. Consider communication skills, client interaction requirements, and personality fit with the project culture.

For that manufacturing project, I needed people who could work independently, communicate clearly with non-technical users, and handle the pressure of a high-visibility implementation. Technical skills were important, but soft skills were equally critical.

I also learned to build redundancy into my team structure. Having only one person who understands a critical piece of the system is dangerous. If that person gets sick, quits, or turns out to be incompetent, you're stuck.

Now I make sure at least two people understand each major component of the project. This costs a bit more upfront but provides insurance against the inevitable personnel problems.

Remote team management adds another layer of complexity. Time zones, communication channels, and relationship-building without physical presence all require deliberate planning. Daily standups, shared documentation, and a real investment in keeping people connected are the basics. It takes more discipline than in-person work, not less.

Managing subcontractors requires a different approach than managing employees. Subcontractors are running their own businesses and have their own priorities. You can't tell them what to do the same way you'd direct an employee.

The key is aligning their business interests with your project goals. Make sure they understand how their success on your project affects their long-term relationship with you and potential for future work. Good subcontractors will go the extra mile if they see the value in maintaining the relationship.

Clear contracts and well-defined deliverables become even more important with subcontractors. You need documented agreements about scope, timeline, quality standards, and payment terms. Misunderstandings that might be easily resolved with employees can turn into legal disputes with subcontractors.

The best team members are the ones you want to work with again and again. When you find good people, take care of them. Pay them fairly, give them interesting work, and maintain relationships between projects. A network of reliable team members is one of the most valuable assets a consultant can have.

I still work regularly with Marcus and Elena from that manufacturing project, now almost 15 years later. We've probably saved each other a combined hundred hours of onboarding friction over the years because we already know how each other works. That relationship started because I stopped treating team-building as an emergency response to a staffing gap and started treating it as something worth investing in while I wasn't desperate. When Kevin showed up unable to connect to a database and Sarah disappeared for days at a stretch, I learned what bad team selection costs. Marcus and Elena are what good team selection pays.

Solo consulting has a ceiling. You can only work so many hours, take on so much scope, absorb so many simultaneous projects. Team-based consulting removes that ceiling. But the team has to actually work — which means vetting people before you need them, building relationships before the deadline pressure hits, and managing each person the way they need to be managed rather than the way is easiest for you.

| 13 |

Remote work considerations

Remote consulting has gone from unusual to standard practice in just a few years. What used to be the exception for distributed teams is now the default for many projects. This shift has created new opportunities and new challenges that every consultant needs to master.

I was forced to learn remote project management during a crisis situation that taught me more about distributed teams than years of traditional consulting. A major client's headquarters got hit by a hurricane that knocked out power and flooded the entire building. The project couldn't stop, but suddenly nobody could work from the office.

Within 48 hours, I had to figure out how to manage a team of twelve people scattered across six states, all working from their homes with varying levels of technology and workspace setup. Half the team had never worked remotely for more than a day. The client's IT infrastructure was a mess. And the project deadline hadn't changed despite the chaos.

That week taught me that remote work isn't just office work done from home. It's a completely different way of managing projects that requires new skills, different tools, and a fundamental shift in how you think about team coordination.

The biggest challenge with remote teams isn't technology, it's trust. When you can't see people working, it's natural to worry about whether they're productive. When team members can't see each other, it's easy for them to feel disconnected and lose motivation.

Trust in a remote environment requires overcommunication and transparency. I started requiring daily check-ins from every team member, not because I didn't trust them, but because everyone needed to feel connected to the project and each other.

These weren't micromanagement sessions. Each person would send a brief email covering what they accomplished yesterday, what they planned to work on today, and any roadblocks they were facing. The whole team could see everyone's updates, creating accountability and helping people coordinate their work.

Remote communication has to be more intentional than office communication. You can't rely on casual conversations by the coffee machine or quick questions while walking past someone's desk. Every interaction has to be planned and initiated deliberately.

I learned to use different communication channels for different purposes. Instant messaging for quick questions and casual coordination. Email for detailed discussions and documentation. Video calls for complex problem-solving and relationship building. Phone calls for sensitive conversations or urgent issues.

The key is establishing protocols that everyone understands. When do you use chat versus email? How quickly should people respond to different types of messages? What constitutes an emergency that justifies interrupting someone outside normal hours?

Video conferencing became essential, and I had to learn fast that remote meetings don't work like in-person ones. Keep them shorter — 30 minutes or less when possible. Break content into segments instead of one long presentation, and call on people by name to keep them from drifting. Invest in a decent headset and a reliable connection. Poor audio kills a remote meeting faster than any agenda problem.

Managing time zones becomes a major consideration when team members are distributed geographically. What seems like a simple scheduling challenge can become a nightmare when you have people in New York, Los Angeles, and London trying to collaborate.

I learned to use shared calendars that show everyone's time zones and availability. I rotate meeting times so that different team members aren't always stuck with early morning or late evening calls. For projects with extreme time zone differences, I sometimes run duplicate meetings to accommodate different regions.

Asynchronous work becomes more important with remote teams. Not everything needs to happen in real-time when people are working across different time zones. I structure projects so that team members can hand off work to each other and make progress even when they're not online at the same time.

This requires better documentation and clearer specifications. When someone finishes a task at 6 PM in California and hands it off to someone starting work at 9 AM in New York, there can't be any ambiguity about what was done and what needs to happen next.

File sharing and version control become critical with remote teams. When everyone is working from different locations with different devices, you need bulletproof systems for managing project files and preventing conflicts.

Cloud-based platforms like Google Drive, Dropbox, or SharePoint solve most of these problems, but you still need clear protocols about folder structure, file naming, and version management. I've seen remote projects grind to a halt because people couldn't find the latest version of a critical document.

Security is where remote work gets unpleasant to think about. When team members are working from home networks, coffee shops, and airport lounges, you can't rely on office network security to protect sensitive client data. A VPN for anyone accessing client systems is non-negotiable, not a suggestion. Encrypt sensitive files. Use file sharing platforms that have explicit data protection agreements. And get this squared away at the start of the project, not after someone asks why you're sending client data over personal Gmail.

Some clients have particular security requirements for remote work that need to be nailed down in the SOW. Government contracts, healthcare projects, and financial services work often have strict rules about where work can be performed and how data must be protected. Find out before you start, not after you've been working from your kitchen table for three weeks.

Relationships become harder but more important with remote teams. People need to trust and like each other to collaborate effectively, but it's much more difficult to develop personal connections when you only interact through screens.

I try to get remote teams together in person at least once during a project, usually at the beginning. A couple of days working face-to-face builds relationships that carry through months of remote collaboration. When in-person meetings aren't possible, I schedule regular video calls that aren't strictly work-focused.

These relationship-building sessions might include virtual coffee breaks, online team lunches, or informal check-ins where people can talk about non-work topics. It sounds silly, but these casual interactions help team members see each other as people instead of just names on a screen.

Client relationships require different approaches in a remote environment. You can't rely on physical presence to build rapport and confidence. Everything has to be communicated more explicitly and demonstrated more clearly.

I increase the frequency of client communication when working remotely. Weekly status updates become twice-weekly updates. Monthly progress meetings become bi-weekly sessions. I want clients to feel even more connected to the project when we're not physically present.

Remote work also creates opportunities that don't exist with traditional consulting. You can access talent from anywhere in the world instead of being limited to your local market. You can work with clients who would never consider hiring consultants who required on-site presence. You can reduce travel costs and time while increasing project profitability.

I've built successful remote relationships with clients I've never met in person. Some of my most profitable projects have been completely remote from start to finish. The key is being intentional about communication, transparent about progress, and professional in all interactions.

Remote consulting isn't going away. The technology will continue to improve, and both clients and consultants are becoming more comfortable with distributed work arrangements. Consultants who master remote project management will have big advantages over those who insist on traditional in-person approaches.

The skills you develop managing remote teams and clients will make you better at all types of consulting. When you learn to communicate clearly, document thoroughly, and build trust without physical presence, you'll find that these abilities improve your in-person projects as well.

Remote consulting requires more discipline than in-person work, not less. The consultants who figure that out early have access to a global market. The ones who don't are competing for local clients only.

| 14 |

Record everything

Documentation separates professional consultants from amateurs. I've seen more projects saved by good records and more careers destroyed by poor documentation than any other single factor. If you take away only one lesson from this book, make it this: write everything down.

Most consultants hate documentation. They see it as bureaucratic busywork that takes time away from "real" work. They're wrong. Documentation is the real work. Everything else is just implementation.

I learned this lesson during a project that should have been straightforward but turned into a legal nightmare. A small software company hired me to build a customer relationship management system. The project went smoothly for the first six weeks. Then the CEO got fired, the new management team came in, and everything went to hell.

The new CEO, a guy named Blackwell, decided he didn't like the direction of the project. He claimed the previous management had never authorized the work I was doing. He said my invoices were fraudulent and threatened to sue me for breach of contract.

I knew this was bullshit. I had email approvals for every phase of the work. I had meeting notes documenting every major decision. I had a signed statement of work that clearly defined the project scope. But when I went to gather this evidence, I discovered a problem.

My documentation was scattered across multiple email accounts, buried in various folders, and mixed up with personal files. Some of the meeting notes were handwritten on random pieces of paper. Key email conversations had been deleted when I cleaned out my inbox. The signed SOW was in a box somewhere in my garage.

It took me three days to assemble a complete picture of what had been agreed to and when. By then, Blackwell had already contacted his lawyer and was threatening a lawsuit. What should have been a simple contract dispute became a months-long legal battle that cost me more in attorney fees than I made on the original project.

That experience taught me that documentation isn't just about covering your ass, although it's certainly useful for that. Good documentation makes projects run more smoothly, prevents misunderstandings, and provides a roadmap for future work.

Now I document everything from the first client conversation through the final project delivery. Not because I expect problems, but because problems are inevitable and preparation is the difference between minor inconveniences and major disasters.

I start documenting before the project even begins. Initial client conversations get summarized in email. Proposal discussions get recorded in meeting notes. Contract negotiations get tracked in a dedicated folder. By the time I sign a contract, I already have a complete history of how the project came together.

During the sales process, I send follow-up emails after every big conversation. Something like: "Thanks for the productive meeting this morning. Just to summarize what we discussed: you need a new inventory system to replace the manual tracking process, the budget is around $15,000, and you want to go live by the end of March. The main concerns you mentioned were data migration from the old system and training for the warehouse staff. Does this capture the key points accurately?"

This serves two purposes. First, it ensures we're both on the same page about requirements and expectations. Second, it creates a written record of what was discussed and agreed upon.

Once the project starts, I maintain several types of documentation: project logs, decision records, communication archives, and deliverable tracking. Each serves a different purpose and together they provide comprehensive coverage of project activities.

The project log is a running diary of events, milestones, and issues. Nothing fancy, just a chronological record of what happened when. I update it weekly with bullet points covering major accomplishments, decisions made, problems encountered, and upcoming activities.

This log becomes invaluable when you need to trace the history of a problem or explain why certain decisions were made. Six months after a project ends, nobody remembers the exact sequence of events that led to a particular choice. The project log provides that context.

Decision records document the reasoning behind major choices. When we decide to use database A instead of database B, I write a brief summary of the options considered, the criteria used to evaluate them, and the factors that drove the final decision.

This prevents second-guessing later in the project. When someone questions why we chose a particular approach, I can point to the documented reasoning instead of trying to reconstruct the thought process from memory.

Communication archives are organized copies of all project-related emails, meeting notes, and formal correspondence. I create dedicated folders for each project and file everything chronologically. Important documents get flagged and cross-referenced for easy retrieval.

Email is your most important communication record, but only if you can find the relevant messages when you need them. I use descriptive subject lines, consistent folder structures, and regular archiving to keep email organized and searchable.

Meeting notes get written during every discussion, whether it's a formal conference room session or a casual phone call. I don't try to capture every word, but I do record decisions made, action items assigned, and any changes to project scope or timeline.

For virtual meetings, I always record the session unless the client asks me not to. Zoom and other platforms make this easy by automatically notifying all participants that the meeting is being recorded. I configure the software to inform everyone when recording starts, preventing any surprises or privacy concerns.

AI tools have made meeting documentation dramatically easier. Tools like Otter.ai, Fireflies, and Zoom's built-in AI summary will transcribe the meeting, identify action items, and produce a searchable record automatically. I still review and clean up the output before sending it to clients — AI transcription stumbles on technical jargon, misidentifies speakers, and occasionally produces a sentence that makes no sense — but it gets you 80% of the way there in about two minutes. That used to take an hour. The recordings get saved to the project folder by date; the transcripts get reviewed and sent to all participants within 24 hours.

Having meeting recordings has saved me more times than I can count. When clients claim they never agreed to something or insist they said the opposite of what happened, the recording ends the argument. I've never had to actually play one back. The fact that they exist is usually enough.

Deliverable tracking documents what was produced, when it was delivered, and how it was received by the client. This covers everything from interim reports to final system implementations. I maintain a simple spreadsheet that shows deliverable name, due date, delivery date, client approval status, and any related issues.

This tracking prevents things from falling through the cracks and provides clear evidence of project progress. When clients question whether milestones are being met, I can show exactly what has been delivered and when.

Change control documentation is critical for managing scope creep and protecting yourself from disputes. Every change request gets documented with a description of the requested modification, impact on timeline and budget, and client approval before any work begins. If a client later claims they never authorized extra work, your signed change orders end that conversation fast.

File organization becomes critical as documentation accumulates. I use a consistent folder structure for every project: contracts and legal documents, correspondence, meeting notes, deliverables, change requests, and administrative files. Files get named with dates first — "2024-03-15 Project Status Meeting Notes.doc" — because that makes them sort correctly and findable six months later when you're trying to reconstruct what happened in March. Inconsistent naming sounds like a minor complaint until you're searching through 400 files trying to find a specific email from a client who's now threatening to sue you.

Everything lives in cloud storage with automatic backup and version history. Legal documents get printed and filed as hard copies too. This is old-fashioned and I don't care — I once spent three days assembling documentation for a contract dispute because my digital records were scattered across multiple accounts. I had the signed SOW. It was in a box in my garage. Hard copies of important contracts now live in a dedicated folder in my filing cabinet. That folder has never been relevant. I intend to keep it that way.

Time tracking records provide another layer of documentation that's valuable for both billing and project analysis. I log time against tasks and project phases, not just total hours worked. This granular tracking helps with future project estimation and provides evidence of work performed if disputes arise.

The time tracking doesn't need to be elaborate. A simple spreadsheet with date, hours, task description, and project phase is sufficient. The key is consistency and detail in the task descriptions.

Financial records tie everything together by providing a paper trail of project costs, payments, and profitability. I track expenses against projects and maintain detailed records of all invoices and payments.

Good financial documentation helps with tax preparation, business analysis, and dispute resolution. It also provides valuable data for improving project estimation and pricing for future work.

The goal isn't to become a documentation bureaucrat who spends more time writing about work than doing work. The goal is to create a comprehensive record that protects your interests, improves project management, and provides valuable historical data.

Start with the basics: project logs, decision records, and communication archives. Add other types of documentation as projects become more complex or risks increase. The investment in documentation time pays dividends in reduced conflicts, smoother project execution, and better business insights.

Remember that documentation is only valuable if you can find and use it when needed. Develop consistent organizational systems and stick to them across all projects. The extra effort required to maintain good records will save you countless hours and potentially thousands of dollars when problems arise.

| 15 |

E&O insurance

Errors and omissions insurance is the one thing standing between you and financial ruin when a consulting project goes badly wrong. Most consultants either skip it entirely or buy inadequate coverage because they think it's expensive and unnecessary. They're wrong on both counts.

I learned about E&O insurance by watching a colleague get destroyed by a lawsuit that should have been manageable. Randy, a database consultant I'd worked with on several projects, was upgrading an inventory management system for a mid-sized manufacturing company. Everything went smoothly for the first two months. Then their accountant discovered a problem.

The new system was calculating inventory values incorrectly due to a rounding error in Randy's code. The mistake was tiny, just a few cents per transaction, but it had been accumulating for weeks. By the time they caught it, their financial statements were off by $47,000.

The client was furious. They'd already filed quarterly reports with the incorrect numbers and had to restate their financials. The accounting firm charged them $12,000 to redo the books. The bank questioned their loan covenants. The CFO got fired, partly because of the mess.

The client sued Randy for $200,000, claiming the error had damaged their reputation and cost them a major contract. They wanted compensation for the accounting fees, legal costs, lost business opportunities, and punitive damages for what they called "gross negligence."

Randy knew the lawsuit was overblown. The rounding error was a simple programming mistake, not negligence. The lost contract probably had nothing to do with the inventory system. But fighting the lawsuit was going to cost more than he could afford, and there was always the risk that a jury might side with the angry client.

That's when Randy discovered he didn't have adequate E&O coverage. He had a basic business liability policy that covered slip-and-fall accidents and property damage, but it excluded professional services errors. His consulting work wasn't covered at all.

Randy ended up settling for $75,000, wiping out two years of profits and nearly putting him out of business. The legal fees alone cost another $25,000. All because of a rounding error that took five minutes to fix once they found it.

Watching Randy go through that nightmare convinced me to get serious about E&O coverage. Now I carry $2 million in E&O insurance and consider it the best money I spend each year. The peace of mind alone is worth the premium, but the coverage has saved me twice when clients made unreasonable claims.

E&O insurance covers professional mistakes that cause financial harm to clients. This covers errors in your work, failure to deliver services as promised, misrepresentation of your capabilities, and breach of professional duties. It doesn't cover intentional wrongdoing, criminal acts, or general business liabilities.

The key word is "professional." If you slip and fall in a client's office, that's general liability. If your code crashes their server and costs them money, that's E&O. If you give bad advice that leads to poor business decisions, that's E&O. If you miss a deadline that causes them to lose a contract, that's probably E&O.

The most important thing to remember about E&O insurance is this: call your insurance company the moment you discover any legal issue. Don't wait, don't try to handle it yourself, and don't ignore threatening letters hoping they'll go away. Your insurance company will assign lawyers to the case and take it over for you.

Randy made the mistake of trying to negotiate with the angry client himself for two weeks before contacting his insurance company. By then, the client had already filed the lawsuit and hired an expensive law firm. If Randy had called his insurance company immediately when the client first threatened legal action, the insurance company's lawyers might have resolved the issue before it became a formal lawsuit.

Coverage limits matter more than you think. A $1 million policy sounds like a lot until you're facing a lawsuit from a Fortune 500 company with deep pockets and expensive lawyers. Legal defense costs alone can easily hit six figures, even if you eventually win the case.

I carry $2 million per claim with a $2 million annual aggregate. This means the insurance company will pay up to $2 million for any single claim and up to $2 million total for all claims in a year. Defense costs usually come out of the policy limits, so you want enough coverage to handle both legal fees and any settlement or judgment.

Deductibles affect both your premiums and your out-of-pocket costs when claims arise. Higher deductibles mean lower premiums but more money out of your pocket if something goes wrong. I carry a $10,000 deductible, keeping my premiums reasonable while ensuring I have skin in the game to avoid frivolous claims.

The insurance company's duty to defend is just as important as their duty to pay damages. Good E&O policies require the insurance company to hire lawyers and defend you against covered claims. This can save you tens of thousands in legal fees even if the claim is ultimately unsuccessful.

Make sure your policy covers defense costs in addition to damages, not as part of the coverage limit. Some policies have "defense costs within limits" language that means legal fees reduce the amount available to pay claims. You want "defense costs in addition to limits" coverage.

Prior acts coverage protects you against claims arising from work done before your policy started. This is critical if you're switching insurance companies or buying E&O coverage for the first time after years of consulting. Without it, you're only covered for new work going forward. I learned about this the hard way when a colleague switched carriers and then got sued three years later over a project he'd done under his old policy. His new carrier declined the claim. He paid out of pocket.

Most E&O policies are claims-made, meaning they only cover claims filed while the policy is active. Let your policy lapse and you're unprotected for work you did when you were covered. Occurrence policies are better — they cover any work done during the policy period regardless of when the claim gets filed — but they cost more. If you can afford occurrence coverage, get it. If not, understand that you need to keep your claims-made policy active continuously.

Read the exclusions before you buy anything. Most policies exclude cyber liability, employment practices, and intellectual property infringement. If you do web development, make sure cyber attacks are covered. If your specialty is healthcare or finance, get a policy designed for consultants in those fields — generic professional liability often has gaps in regulated industries. And on the application, describe what you actually do. If you describe yourself as a basic database consultant and then take on complex enterprise architecture work, the insurer can deny coverage when something goes wrong.

Premiums are $500–1,500 per year for $1–2 million in coverage depending on your risk profile. Technology consulting costs more than general business consulting. A single day in court with a good lawyer costs more than your annual premium. It's also tax-deductible. Large corporate and government clients will often require proof of coverage and want to be named as additional insureds before they'll sign anything — budget a few days to get certificates processed when that comes up.

When something goes wrong: call your insurance company first, before you talk to the client again. Don't admit fault, don't discuss settlement numbers, don't try to negotiate it yourself. The insurer has people who do this professionally. Multiple claims — even ones they pay out — can make you uninsurable or spike your premiums. Let the professionals manage it.

Don't wait until you need it to buy E&O coverage. Insurance companies won't sell you a policy after a claim has been filed, and prior acts coverage might not protect work done before you had any coverage. Buy it early in your consulting career and maintain continuous coverage.

Shop around for E&O coverage but focus on coverage quality instead of just price. The cheapest policy is worthless if it doesn't cover your actual consulting work or if the insurance company fights every claim. Work with agents who understand consulting businesses and can explain policy differences.

E&O insurance is one of the best investments you can make in your consulting practice. It protects your personal assets, gives you peace of mind, and demonstrates professionalism to clients. The cost is reasonable compared to the protection it provides.

Don't learn about E&O insurance by watching a colleague get destroyed. Get covered before you need it, carry adequate limits, and sleep better knowing that a simple mistake won't destroy your business or your financial future.

| 16 |

Demand respect and treat with respect

Respect is the foundation of every successful consulting relationship. Without mutual respect, projects turn into power struggles, communication breaks down, and outcomes suffer. The key is establishing respect from the first interaction and maintaining it throughout the engagement.

Most consultants make the mistake of tolerating disrespect because they're afraid of losing clients or creating conflict. This approach backfires because you train clients by what you tolerate. If you accept rude behavior, unreasonable demands, or unprofessional treatment early in the relationship, it will only get worse.

I learned this lesson during a project with a tech startup where the CEO had a habit of interrupting meetings to take phone calls, showing up late to scheduled discussions, and making dismissive comments about my recommendations. I initially overlooked these behaviors because the project was lucrative and I didn't want to create tension.

The disrespect escalated quickly. The CEO started questioning my expertise in front of other team members, making jokes about my fees, and treating me like a junior employee instead of a professional consultant. By the time I realized the relationship had become toxic, the pattern was so established that addressing it felt awkward and confrontational.

The project became a nightmare. Every meeting turned into a debate. Simple decisions required multiple discussions. The CEO's attitude infected the rest of the team, who began treating me with similar disrespect. I eventually completed the technical work, but the relationship was so damaged that they refused to provide references or consider me for future projects.

That experience taught me that addressing disrespect immediately is essential for maintaining professional relationships. The time to handle inappropriate behavior is the moment it happens, not after it becomes a pattern. Waiting only makes the problem worse and harder to resolve.

Now I address disrespect directly and professionally as soon as it occurs. If a client interrupts me repeatedly during a presentation, I stop and say, "I'd like to finish explaining this concept before we move to questions." If someone makes dismissive comments about my recommendations, I respond with, "I'd appreciate if we could discuss the technical merits instead of dismissing the approach."

The key is being assertive without being hostile. Assertiveness means standing up for yourself and maintaining professional boundaries. Hostility means attacking or retaliating against the other person. The goal is to address the behavior while preserving the working relationship.

Assertive responses focus on the behavior instead of attacking the person's character. Instead of saying, "You're being rude," I might say, "I need to be able to complete my thoughts before we discuss alternatives." Instead of, "You never listen to me," I say, "Let's make sure we understand each other's perspectives on this issue."

Body language and tone matter as much as words when addressing disrespect. I maintain calm, professional demeanor while being clear about my expectations. Raised voices, aggressive postures, or defensive reactions escalate conflicts instead of resolving them. The goal is to be firm but not combative.

Some clients test consultants early in the relationship to establish dominance or gauge how they'll be treated. These tests might involve unreasonable demands, rude comments, or attempts to renegotiate agreed-upon terms. How you respond to these early tests sets the tone for the entire engagement.

I've had clients try to add scope to projects during kickoff meetings, expecting me to absorb the extra work without additional compensation. I address these attempts immediately by referring back to our signed agreement and explaining that scope changes require formal approval and additional fees.

Other clients try to establish power dynamics by making consultants wait for meetings, canceling at the last minute, or treating consulting time as less valuable than their own time. I address schedule disrespect by implementing policies about meeting confirmations, cancellation notice, and rescheduling fees.

The consulting relationship works best when both parties treat each other as professionals. I maintain high standards for my own behavior — I arrive early, come prepared, follow through on commitments, and communicate proactively. That sets a standard that makes it easier to expect the same from clients.

Boundary setting is non-negotiable. Establish your business hours, response time expectations, and emergency protocols at the start of every engagement. When clients contact you outside those boundaries, respond professionally but reinforce the protocol. Don't let schedule disrespect become a habit — once you start taking calls at 10 PM, you'll be taking them every week. A server failure is an emergency. A presentation someone forgot about is not.

When clients try to renegotiate your fees mid-project, refer back to the agreement and hold the line. When team members undermine the engagement, escalate to the primary client — that's their problem to manage, not yours. When behavior that looks like disrespect might actually be cultural difference, research before you react. And when a client persistently violates professional boundaries despite direct conversation about it, the right answer is often to end the engagement.

The short-term loss is always smaller than the long-term damage of a toxic client relationship.

Remember that you train clients by what you tolerate. If you accept disrespectful behavior early in the relationship, it will become the standard for all future interactions. Address problems immediately, maintain professional boundaries, and demand the same level of respect that you provide to clients.

Mutual respect isn't just nice to have in consulting relationships, it's essential for project success. Invest in establishing and maintaining respect from the first client interaction, and you'll build a consulting practice based on professional partnerships instead of adversarial relationships.

| 17 |

When it goes south

Projects go bad despite your best efforts. When that happens, how you handle the crisis determines whether you salvage the relationship, protect your reputation, and minimize financial damage, or whether you turn a manageable problem into a complete disaster.

I learned about crisis management by watching a colleague handle a project that started well but deteriorated into the worst professional experience I'd ever witnessed. A regional insurance company hired Derek, a systems consultant I knew, to upgrade their claims processing system, a six-month project worth $80,000. The initial requirements were clear, the client seemed professional, and the technical work was within his expertise.

Three months into the project, everything started falling apart. The client's IT director, who had been Derek's primary contact, left the company unexpectedly. His replacement had different ideas about the system requirements and wanted to change the database structure Derek had already implemented. The new IT director also questioned every design decision Derek had made and demanded explanations for choices that had been previously approved.

Meanwhile, the claims processing software vendor released a major update that broke compatibility with Derek's integration code. The client's management began pressuring for faster delivery because they were facing a regulatory audit. The project timeline compressed from six months to four months, but the scope kept expanding as different departments added their own requirements.

Derek made several critical mistakes in handling these cascading problems. He tried to accommodate every request to keep the client happy. He worked longer hours to meet the compressed timeline without renegotiating the contract. He absorbed the extra costs of redesigning the database structure instead of demanding payment for additional work.

Most importantly, Derek failed to communicate the severity of the problems to senior management. He kept hoping he could solve the technical issues and make up for lost time, so he minimized the problems in his status reports. By the time the client realized how far behind the project had fallen, they blamed him for failing to deliver on schedule.

The project ultimately failed. Derek delivered a working system, but it was three months late and missing several features that had been added to the scope during development. The client refused to pay the final $20,000, claiming breach of contract. They also threatened to sue him for the costs of hiring another consultant to complete the missing features.

Watching Derek's disaster taught me that early intervention is crucial when projects start going sideways. The longer you wait to address problems, the more difficult they become to solve and the more likely they are to damage your professional relationships.

Now I watch for early warning signs that projects are heading toward trouble. Scope creep, timeline pressure, personnel changes, and communication breakdowns all signal potential problems that need immediate attention.

The first warning sign is usually scope expansion without corresponding timeline or budget adjustments. Clients start asking for "small additions" or "minor enhancements" that seem reasonable individually but add up to big extra work. These requests often come during casual conversations instead of formal change control processes.

I've learned to stop work immediately when scope changes aren't properly documented and approved. A simple email to the client saying "I want to confirm that the additional reporting features we discussed will add approximately 15 hours to the project timeline and $2,250 to the cost" forces them to acknowledge the scope change and its impact.

Communication changes often signal deeper problems. When your primary contact stops responding quickly to emails, starts missing scheduled meetings, or begins delegating communications to subordinates, something has changed in their priorities or authority.

I pay attention to the tone and content of client communications. Short, terse responses that used to be friendly and detailed suggest frustration or pressure. Requests for excessive documentation or justification of routine decisions indicate loss of trust or confidence.

Personnel changes create immediate risks because new people don't understand the project history or previous decisions. When key stakeholders leave or get reassigned, you need to quickly establish relationships with their replacements and ensure they understand the project scope and status.

I schedule introduction meetings with new team members within 48 hours of learning about personnel changes. These meetings cover project background, current status, upcoming milestones, and any decisions that need their input. I also provide them with copies of all relevant documentation and previous meeting notes.

Timeline pressure often comes from external factors like regulatory requirements, budget cycles, or management demands. Clients who previously seemed reasonable about deadlines suddenly want everything delivered faster without reducing scope or adding resources.

When clients request timeline acceleration, I provide analysis of what's possible and what's not. If they want to compress a six-month project into four months, I explain which features could be delayed, what additional resources would be needed, or what risks they'd be accepting.

Budget constraints can signal financial problems that affect your payment. Clients who start questioning routine expenses, requesting detailed cost justifications, or asking about payment deferrals may be having cash flow problems.

I investigate immediately when clients show signs of financial stress. This might involve checking their public financial reports, talking to other vendors, or simply asking direct questions about payment timing and budget availability.

Quality complaints that seem disproportionate to actual problems often indicate unrealistic expectations or hidden agendas. When clients find fault with work that meets the agreed-upon requirements, they may be setting up justification for scope changes or payment disputes.

I respond to quality concerns by referring back to the original requirements and demonstrating how the delivered work meets those requirements. If clients want different functionality, that becomes a change request instead of a quality issue.

Political changes within client organizations can kill projects even when the technical work is going well. New management, budget cuts, strategic shifts, or reorganizations can eliminate support for your project regardless of its value or progress.

I try to stay informed about client organization changes through informal conversations and industry news. When I learn about management changes or strategic shifts, I assess how they might affect my project and prepare contingency plans.

The key to managing project crises is early escalation to appropriate stakeholders. When problems arise, I communicate immediately with the people who have authority to make decisions about scope, timeline, or budget. Waiting and hoping problems will resolve themselves usually makes situations worse.

My escalation process covers documenting the problem clearly, analyzing the impact on project deliverables and timeline, proposing solutions with associated costs, and requesting decisions by deadlines.

This approach forces clients to acknowledge problems and make informed choices about how to proceed.

Sometimes the best solution is stopping work temporarily until problems can be resolved. I've learned that continuing to work during major scope or timeline disputes usually creates more problems than it solves. It's better to pause the project, resolve the underlying issues, and then restart with clear expectations.

The mechanics of stopping work matter as much as the decision to stop. Send a written notice to the client explaining that you are pausing work pending resolution of the specified issue — name the issue specifically, don't be vague. Invoice for all work completed to that date and make clear the invoice is due under existing contract terms regardless of the dispute. Keep your tone professional and factual. Don't threaten, don't explain at length, don't apologize. State what you've done, what you're owed, and what needs to be resolved before work resumes. Clients who were acting in bad faith often pay quickly when they realize you're serious. Clients who were acting in good faith appreciate the clarity.

When projects can't be salvaged, I focus on minimizing damage to my reputation and financial exposure. This might involve negotiating partial payments for completed work, documenting the reasons for project failure, or agreeing to mutual termination instead of continuing an unwinnable situation.

I always conduct post-mortem analysis after troubled projects. Not the formal kind where everyone sits in a room and pretends everything was a learning experience — the honest kind where I write down what I actually got wrong and what I'd do differently. I keep these notes. Years later, when a new project starts showing similar warning signs, I can go back and see that I've been here before.

Documentation during a crisis matters more than documentation during smooth sailing, because memories get unreliable fast when the pressure is on and people have reasons to remember things conveniently. Keep records of every communication, every scope discussion, every decision. Not to build a legal case — to have accurate information. If you end up in a dispute, you want to be the one who knows exactly what happened.

Get a lawyer on the phone early when something is heading toward a dispute — before you send another email to the client, before you agree to anything, before you decide the situation doesn't warrant it. An hour of legal consultation costs less than a day in court, and a good attorney can often tell you in that hour whether you have a real problem or whether a firmly worded letter will end it. I've called mine three times. Once it cost me an hour's fee and saved me a lawsuit. Twice he told me I was overreacting. Either way it was worth it.

The goal of crisis management isn't to win every dispute or salvage every troubled project. It's to protect your business interests while maintaining professional relationships where possible. Sometimes walking away from a bad situation is the best decision for long-term success.

Learn to recognize the early warning signs of troubled projects, and you'll be able to intervene before problems become disasters. Develop systematic approaches to crisis communication and escalation, and you'll handle the inevitable problems that arise in consulting work.

Project failures are part of the consulting business, but how you handle them determines whether they become learning experiences that strengthen your practice or disasters that damage your reputation and financial stability.

| 18 |

Advanced stakeholder management

Managing stakeholders becomes exponentially more complex as you move up the organizational hierarchy. The skills that work with middle managers fail spectacularly with executives. The communication style that builds trust with technical teams can alienate board members. Understanding these differences is essential for consulting success at the enterprise level.

I learned about executive stakeholder management during a project that nearly ended my relationship with a major client. A Fortune 500 manufacturing company hired me to design a new inventory management system. The technical work was straightforward, but the project required approval from the executive team for a $2 million implementation budget.

My primary contact was the IT director, a technically savvy guy who understood databases and appreciated detailed explanations of system architecture. We worked well together, and he was enthusiastic about the proposed solution. When it came time to present to the executive team, he suggested I give the same technical presentation that had convinced him.

I walked into the boardroom with 40 slides covering database schemas, integration patterns, and performance benchmarks. The executives looked bored after the first five slides and started checking their phones after ten slides. By slide 20, the CEO interrupted me and asked, "How much will this cost and what problems will it solve?"

I tried to explain the technical benefits: faster query performance, better data integrity, improved scalability. The executives exchanged glances that clearly said "this guy doesn't get it." The CFO asked how the new system would reduce operating costs. The head of operations wanted to know how it would improve customer satisfaction. I had no good answers because I'd focused entirely on technical details.

The presentation was a disaster. The executive team approved a much smaller budget for a limited pilot project instead of the full implementation we'd proposed. Worse, they lost confidence in my ability to understand their business needs, affecting my relationship with the company for years.

That experience taught me that different stakeholders care about completely different things. Technical people want to understand how systems work. Middle managers want to know how changes will affect their daily operations. Executives want to understand business impact, financial returns, and strategic advantages.

Now I prepare different presentations for different audiences, even when discussing the same project. The technical deep-dive that impresses IT staff gets condensed into three bullet points for executives. The detailed implementation timeline that project managers love becomes a high-level milestone chart for senior leadership.

Executive presentations focus on business outcomes instead of technical features. Instead of explaining database optimization techniques, I talk about faster customer response times. Instead of describing integration architectures, I highlight reduced manual work and improved accuracy. Instead of detailing security protocols, I emphasize compliance and risk reduction.

The key is translating technical work into business language that executives understand and care about. A new reporting system doesn't matter because it uses modern technology. It matters because it gives managers better visibility into operations, enables faster decision-making, and reduces the time spent on manual data compilation.

Board-level presentations require even more abstraction from technical details. Board members have limited time and want to understand strategic implications instead of implementation details. They care about competitive advantages, return on investment, and risks to the organization.

I structure board presentations around three questions: What problem are we solving? How will this solution benefit the organization? What are the risks and mitigation strategies? Everything else is supporting detail that should be available if requested but not included in the main presentation.

Political navigation becomes critical when stakeholders have competing agendas or conflicting priorities. Different departments often want different things from the same project, and executives may have personal interests that don't align with organizational goals.

I learned about corporate politics during a project where the head of sales and the head of operations had fundamentally different views about a new customer management system. Sales wanted features that would help them track prospects and manage the sales pipeline. Operations wanted functionality that would streamline order processing and customer service.

Both executives had valid requirements, but implementing everything would have doubled the project cost and timeline. They each lobbied for their priorities and tried to get me to advocate for their position with senior management. I made the mistake of trying to please both of them by promising to include all their requirements.

The project scope expanded beyond what was technically feasible within the approved budget. When I had to tell them that some features would need to be delayed, both executives blamed me for poor planning and inadequate technical expertise. I had gotten caught in the middle of their political conflict instead of forcing them to resolve their competing priorities.

Now I identify stakeholder conflicts early and escalate resolution to appropriate levels instead of trying to manage competing demands myself. When department heads have conflicting requirements, I document both positions and ask senior leadership to prioritize them. I don't take sides or promise impossible solutions.

Managing up requires understanding how your direct contacts fit into the larger organizational structure. Your primary contact might be enthusiastic about the project, but their boss might have different priorities. Their boss's boss might be focused on completely different strategic initiatives.

I always ask about approval chains and decision-making processes during project planning. Who needs to sign off on major deliverables? Who controls the budget? Who has veto authority over project decisions? These relationships help me navigate organizational politics and ensure the right people are informed and engaged.

Communication frequency and format need to be customized for different stakeholder levels. Technical staff often want detailed weekly updates covering tasks and milestones. Middle managers prefer summary reports that highlight progress and flag issues requiring their attention. Executives want monthly overviews that focus on schedule, budget, and business impact.

I create different reporting templates for different audiences and automate as much of the routine reporting as possible. Technical status reports might be three pages of detailed task updates. Executive summaries are one page with bullet points covering key accomplishments, upcoming milestones, and any issues requiring leadership attention.

Crisis communication requires care when managing senior stakeholders. Executives hate surprises and want to hear about problems before they affect project outcomes or organizational performance. But they also don't want to be bothered with every minor issue that arises during implementation.

I've developed escalation criteria that help me decide when to communicate problems upward. Technical issues that can be resolved within normal project buffers don't require executive attention. Problems that might affect timeline, budget, or deliverable quality get escalated immediately with proposed solutions and impact analysis.

The format of crisis communication matters as much as the content. Executives want to understand the problem, the impact, the proposed solution, and the timeline for resolution. They don't want to hear about the technical details that caused the problem or the various options that were considered and rejected.

Cultural differences become more pronounced at executive levels because senior leaders often have strong personalities and communication preferences. Some executives want detailed data to support every recommendation. Others prefer high-level concepts and get impatient with too much detail.

I pay attention to executive communication styles during initial meetings and adjust my approach accordingly. Data-driven leaders get presentations with charts, metrics, and quantitative analysis. Big-picture thinkers get strategic overviews with minimal technical detail. Process-oriented executives want to understand implementation steps and risk mitigation strategies.

International stakeholder management adds layers of cultural complexity that can derail projects if not handled carefully. Communication styles, decision-making processes, and business etiquette vary between cultures, and assumptions based on your local experience often don't apply.

I've learned to research cultural business practices before engaging with international stakeholders and to ask local contacts about appropriate communication protocols. Some cultures expect formal, hierarchical communications. Others prefer informal, collaborative discussions. Some value direct feedback. Others consider direct criticism to be disrespectful.

Time zone coordination becomes a major challenge when stakeholders are distributed globally. Finding meeting times that work for people in New York, London, and Singapore requires compromise from everyone involved. But asking senior executives to join calls at inconvenient times can damage relationships.

I try to rotate meeting times for recurring communications so that different stakeholders take turns with early morning or late evening calls. For critical decisions that require input from globally distributed executives, I sometimes run multiple meetings to accommodate different time zones instead of forcing everyone into one difficult time slot.

Stakeholder expectations need to be managed proactively because different people often have different assumptions about project scope, timeline, and deliverables. These misaligned expectations become major problems when they surface late in the project, especially if they involve senior stakeholders.

I document stakeholder expectations explicitly during project planning and review them regularly throughout the engagement. This covers not just functional requirements but also assumptions about communication frequency, decision-making authority, and success criteria.

The goal of advanced stakeholder management isn't to manipulate or deceive people into supporting your project. It's to understand their perspectives, communicate effectively in terms they value, and build relationships that enable project success.

When executives trust your judgment, the work gets easier and the fees get higher. When they don't, every decision goes through three extra layers of approval. Learning to speak their language is worth the effort.

Knowing how to work with executives, navigate corporate politics, and manage complex stakeholder relationships is what separates strategic consultants from technical implementers. Invest in developing these skills, and you'll unlock opportunities for more rewarding and profitable consulting work.

| 19 |

Outsourcing

Outsourcing parts of your consulting projects can be the difference between profitable growth and burnout. The key is knowing what to outsource, when to do it, and how to manage the process without losing control of quality or client relationships.

Most consultants resist outsourcing because they think it means admitting they can't handle the work themselves. That's backwards thinking. Smart outsourcing means recognizing that your time is better spent on high-value activities while delegating routine tasks to people who can do them faster and cheaper.

I learned about outsourcing during a project that nearly killed me. A regional bank hired me to upgrade their entire loan processing system. The scope included database design, application development, user interface creation, data migration, testing, training, and documentation. The timeline was aggressive and the budget was tight.

Three weeks into the project, I was working 16-hour days and falling behind schedule. The database work was going fine because that's my strength, but I was struggling with the user interface design and moving like molasses on the documentation. I'm a decent writer, but creating user manuals and training materials takes me forever.

That's when I realized I was being an idiot. I was spending $150-per-hour time on tasks that could be done by people charging $25-50 per hour. Meanwhile, the high-value database and integration work that only I could do was getting delayed because I was bogged down in routine tasks.

I found a freelance technical writer who worked on software documentation. For $40 per hour, she could create user manuals and training materials faster and better than I could. I hired a user interface designer who charged $75 per hour and could build screens in half the time it took me.

The project turned around immediately. I focused on the database architecture and integration challenges while my outsourced team handled the documentation and interface work. We delivered on time, under budget, and the client was thrilled with the results.

That experience taught me that outsourcing isn't about cutting costs, although it often does that. It's about optimizing the use of your time and skills to deliver better results for clients.

Now I outsource anything that doesn't require my direct expertise or client relationship management. Routine programming, graphic design, content writing, data entry, testing, and documentation all get outsourced to people who can do the work faster and often better than I can.

The key is identifying your core competencies and protecting those while farming out everything else. My core competencies are system architecture, database design, and client relationship management. Everything else is fair game for outsourcing.

Start by making a list of all the tasks involved in your typical project. Then categorize them into three groups: must do myself, could outsource, and should definitely outsource. Be honest about what you're good at and what you hate doing.

Tasks in the "must do myself" category usually involve direct client interaction, major technical decisions, or knowledge that would be difficult to transfer. Client meetings, system architecture, project planning, and final quality reviews typically fall into this category.

The "could outsource" category covers tasks that you can do well but that don't require your unique expertise. Code development, graphic design, content creation, and testing often fit here. Whether you outsource these depends on your workload, timeline, and budget.

The "should definitely outsource" category covers tasks that you're not good at, don't enjoy, or that take you much longer than they should. For me, this covers user interface design, technical writing, and detailed testing. I can do these things, but other people can do them faster and better.

Finding good outsourcing partners takes time and effort, but it's worth the investment. Start by asking other consultants for referrals. Check freelancing websites like Upwork, Freelancer, and Toptal. Look for local talent through networking groups and professional associations.

Don't hire based on price alone. A cheap freelancer who delivers poor work or misses deadlines will cost you more than an expensive one who gets things right the first time. Look for people with relevant experience, good communication skills, and a track record of meeting commitments.

I always start new outsourcing relationships with small test projects. Something that takes 10-20 hours and isn't critical to the main project timeline. This gives me a chance to evaluate their work quality, communication style, and reliability without risking a major deliverable.

The test project also helps establish working procedures and communication protocols. How do they prefer to receive requirements? What format works best for deliverables? How often do they provide status updates? What happens if problems arise?

Clear communication is essential for successful outsourcing. You can't manage outsourced work the same way you manage your own tasks. Everything has to be more explicit and documented because the other person doesn't have the context and background knowledge that you do.

I create detailed specifications for all outsourced work. Not just high-level requirements, but details about format, style, functionality, and quality standards. I include examples of what I want and examples of what I don't want. I cover deadlines, communication expectations, and review procedures.

This level of detail might seem excessive, but it prevents misunderstandings and reduces the need for revisions. An hour spent writing clear specifications saves hours of back-and-forth communication and rework later.

Regular check-ins keep outsourced projects on track. I don't micromanage, but I do want frequent status updates and early visibility into any problems. For short projects, this might mean daily email updates. For longer projects, weekly progress calls work better.

The check-ins should cover progress against milestones, any issues or roadblocks, and upcoming deliverables. I also use these conversations to provide feedback and course corrections before work gets too far down the wrong path.

Quality control becomes more challenging with outsourced work. You need to build review and approval processes into your timeline and budget. Plan for at least one round of revisions on any outsourced deliverable, and budget time for integration and testing.

I always review outsourced work before it goes to the client. This gives me a chance to catch problems, request changes, and ensure that everything meets my quality standards. The client should never know that parts of the project were outsourced unless you choose to tell them.

Managing client expectations around outsourcing requires careful thought. Some clients are fine with outsourcing as long as the work gets done well. Others want to know that you're personally handling every aspect of their project.

I don't hide the fact that I use outsourcing, but I don't advertise it either. I focus on deliverables and results instead of who did the work. If clients ask directly, I'm honest about my use of people for certain tasks while emphasizing that I maintain overall responsibility for quality and project management.

Payment and contract issues get more complex with outsourcing. You need to decide whether to pay outsourced resources directly or have the client contract with them separately. Each approach has advantages and risks.

I prefer to pay outsourced resources myself and bill the client for the total project cost. This gives me more control over the work and keeps the client relationship simple. But it also means I'm responsible for the financial risk if outsourced work needs to be redone or if the client doesn't pay.

For large outsourcing components, I sometimes have the client contract directly with the person while I manage the work. This reduces my financial exposure but can complicate project coordination and communication.

Build a network of reliable outsourcing partners gradually. When you find good people, maintain relationships with them even between projects. Send them occasional work to keep the relationship active. Refer other clients to them when appropriate. Good outsourcing partners are valuable business assets.

I have a core group of five freelancers who I work with regularly: a technical writer, a graphic designer, a user interface developer, a quality assurance specialist, and a general programmer. These people know my standards, understand my communication style, and can jump into new projects quickly.

AI has shifted some of what I used to outsource. First-draft documentation, basic report formatting, initial research on a topic I'm not familiar with — those used to go to freelancers. Now I handle a lot of that myself with AI tools faster than I could brief a freelancer and review their work. This isn't putting people out of business; it's freeing up my outsourcing budget for the work that actually needs human judgment — design decisions, technical nuance, client-facing communication. Periodically reassess what you're outsourcing. Some of it may have a faster path now.

Outsourcing allows you to take on larger, more complex projects than you could handle alone. It also helps smooth out workload variations by giving you flexibility to scale up and down as needed. Most importantly, it frees you to focus on the high-value activities that clients pay premium rates for.

Start small with outsourcing and build your capabilities gradually. Don't try to outsource half your project on the first attempt. Pick one routine task that you hate doing and find someone else to handle it. Learn from that experience before expanding to other areas.

Your time is either spent on work only you can do, or it's wasted. Outsourcing isn't a shortcut. It's how you stop being the bottleneck in your own business.

| 20 |

Using VAs

Virtual assistants can transform your consulting practice by handling routine tasks that eat up your billable hours. The key is understanding what to delegate, how to find good VAs, and how to manage remote workers you've never met in person.

I resisted using virtual assistants for years because I thought it would be more trouble than it was worth. How could someone who'd never worked in my industry understand my clients' needs? How could I trust important tasks to someone in another country? How could I manage someone I couldn't see?

My perspective changed during a project that was drowning me in administrative work. A financial services company hired me to implement a new reporting system that required migrating data from twelve different legacy systems. The technical work was challenging and interesting, but it came with mountains of documentation, data entry, and routine formatting tasks.

I was spending four hours a day on stuff that had nothing to do with my core expertise. Copying data between spreadsheets, formatting reports, creating PowerPoint presentations, and updating project tracking documents. I was billing $150 per hour for consulting work while wasting time on tasks that anyone with basic computer skills could do.

That's when I decided to experiment with a virtual assistant. I found someone through an online platform who worked on data entry and document formatting. She was based in the Philippines, charged $8 per hour, and had excellent reviews from other clients.

The first week was rough. Everything took longer to explain than to do myself. I spent hours creating detailed instructions for simple tasks. I had to review and correct most of her work. I wondered if I was making a mistake.

But by the second week, things started clicking. She understood my formatting preferences, knew how to access the client's systems, and was completing tasks faster than I could. By the end of the month, she was handling 20 hours per week of routine work.

The math was compelling, but not in the way you might think. I paid her $160 per week for work that would have taken me 20 hours to complete myself. I don't bill clients for VA time - this is administrative overhead that I absorb. But by delegating those routine tasks, I freed up 20 hours per week to focus on billable consulting work that only I could do.

The real value isn't in marking up VA costs to clients. It's in using VAs to eliminate non-billable administrative work so you can spend more time on the high-value consulting activities that clients pay premium rates for.

Since then, I've hired VAs from all over the world. I've worked with people from the US, India, Pakistan, Argentina, the Philippines, and many other countries. Each brought different skills, time zones, and cost structures to my projects.

You can save a lot of money by looking outside the US for VA services. American VAs typically charge $15-40 per hour for routine tasks. VAs from countries like the Philippines, India, or Argentina often charge $5-15 per hour for the same quality work. The savings add up quickly when you're delegating 10-20 hours per week.

The time zone differences can work in your favor. When I finish work at 6 PM Pacific time, my VA in the Philippines is starting her day. She can work on tasks overnight and have results waiting when I check email in the morning. This creates a 24-hour work cycle that accelerates project timelines.

Language and communication skills vary between VAs. Don't assume that someone from a particular country will have good or bad English skills. Test communication abilities during the interview process and start with small projects to evaluate their understanding of instructions.

I've found that many VAs from the Philippines, India, and Pakistan have excellent English skills and understand American business practices. VAs from Latin America often have strong technical skills and can work during overlapping US business hours. European VAs typically charge more but offer expertise in particular industries.

The key is matching the VA's skills and cost to your needs. For basic data entry and formatting, cost is the primary factor. For client communication or technical work, language skills and experience become more important. For tasks requiring domain knowledge, you might need to pay premium rates for someone with relevant experience.

Finding good VAs requires patience and a systematic approach. Start with established platforms like Upwork, Freelancer, or Belay that provide ratings, reviews, and payment protection. Look for VAs who work in your type of tasks instead of generalists who claim to do everything.

Read their profiles carefully and pay attention to their work history, client feedback, and communication style. Someone with 50 five-star reviews and detailed client testimonials is a safer bet than someone with no track record, regardless of their claimed experience.

The interview process should test both technical skills and communication abilities. Give them a small paid test project that's similar to the work you'll be delegating. This reveals their capabilities, work quality, and reliability better than any interview question.

I always start new VAs with 5-10 hour test projects that aren't critical to my main client work. Something like reformatting a document, creating a simple spreadsheet, or researching contact information. This gives me a low-risk way to evaluate their skills and working style.

Clear communication is essential for successful VA relationships. You can't manage remote workers the same way you manage local employees. Everything has to be more explicit, detailed, and documented because VAs don't have the context and background knowledge that you do.

I create detailed process documents for all routine tasks that I plan to delegate. These cover step-by-step instructions, quality standards, deadlines, and communication expectations. The upfront investment in documentation pays off through reduced training time and fewer errors.

Screenshots and video recordings are helpful for explaining complex tasks. Instead of writing three pages of instructions for a software process, I record a 5-minute screen capture showing exactly what I want done. This eliminates misunderstandings and speeds up training.

AI tools have made creating VA training materials significantly faster. Tools like Loom combined with AI transcription can turn a screen recording into a written procedure document automatically. AI writing tools can convert rough notes into clean step-by-step instructions a VA can follow without coming back with questions. The time you invest upfront building these materials pays back every time you bring someone new onto a task — instead of re-explaining from scratch, you hand them the document.

Regular check-ins keep VA relationships on track without micromanaging. I schedule weekly calls with new VAs and monthly calls with experienced ones. These conversations cover upcoming projects, process improvements, and any issues or questions.

The check-ins also help build relationships and trust. VAs who feel valued and appreciated do better work and stay with you longer. Treat them as professional partners instead of disposable contractors.

Quality control becomes more important when work is done remotely. Build review and approval processes into your workflow and budget time for checking VA output before it goes to clients. Plan for at least one round of revisions on new types of tasks.

I never send VA work directly to clients without reviewing it first. This protects both my reputation and the client relationship. VAs understand this arrangement and expect feedback that helps them improve their work quality.

Payment and contract terms should be clear from the beginning. Most VA platforms handle payments automatically, but you still need to establish expectations about deadlines, revisions, and scope changes. I prefer weekly payments for ongoing work and milestone payments for project-based tasks.

Time tracking becomes critical for hourly work. Most VAs use time tracking software that captures screenshots and activity levels. This provides transparency for both parties and helps identify productivity issues.

Some clients want to know about your use of VAs, especially for tasks that might involve their confidential information. I include language in my contracts that allows for the use of qualified subcontractors while maintaining my responsibility for all deliverables.

A reliable VA team takes time to build, but the value is real. I now have five VAs who I work with regularly, each handling different types of tasks. This gives me the flexibility to scale up quickly for large projects or handle multiple clients simultaneously.

The VAs know my standards, understand my clients' needs, and can jump into new projects with minimal training. They've become an extension of my consulting practice instead of just temporary help.

Start small with VA delegation and build your capabilities gradually. Pick one routine task that you hate doing and find a VA to handle it. Learn from that experience before expanding to other areas. Not every task is suitable for delegation, and not every VA will be a good fit for your working style.

The goal isn't to delegate everything, but to optimize your time allocation. Focus your energy on high-value activities that require your expertise while outsourcing routine tasks that others can do faster and cheaper.

There's a point in every successful consulting practice where you hit a ceiling on what one person can do. VAs push that ceiling up. If your bottleneck is administrative time, the solution is sitting right there.

The global talent pool is vast and affordable. Take advantage of it to grow your consulting practice beyond what you can accomplish alone.

| 21 |

Using AI for your projects

Artificial intelligence has gone from science fiction novelty to everyday business tool in the span of just a few years. As a consultant, you need to understand how AI can make your projects more efficient, where it falls short, and how to manage client expectations around its use.

I started experimenting with AI tools during a project for a healthcare company that needed their patient data migrated from an ancient system to a modern database. The old system had decades of inconsistent data entry, abbreviations, and formatting quirks that would have taken weeks to clean up manually.

Instead of spending countless hours writing data transformation scripts, I used AI to analyze patterns in the messy data and generate cleaning rules. What would have been three weeks of tedious programming became two days of AI-assisted analysis and validation. The client got cleaner data faster, and I saved time for more valuable activities.

But AI isn't magic, and it's not appropriate for every situation. The key is understanding where AI adds genuine value versus where it creates more problems than it solves.

AI excels at pattern recognition, content generation, data analysis, and routine automation. It's terrible at understanding context, making nuanced judgments, and handling edge cases. Use it for tasks that involve processing large amounts of structured information or generating first drafts of standard content.

I use AI for code generation when I'm working in programming languages I don't use regularly. Instead of spending hours researching syntax and best practices, I can describe what I need and get working code in minutes. The AI-generated code isn't perfect, but it gives me a solid starting point that I can refine and customize.

AI is also useful for documentation tasks. Writing user manuals, technical documentation, and project reports involves a lot of standard language and formatting. AI can generate first drafts that capture the basic structure and content, which I then edit for accuracy and client details.

Data analysis is another area where AI shines. When clients hand me spreadsheets with thousands of rows of transaction data or survey responses, AI can quickly identify trends, outliers, and patterns that would take hours to find manually. This gives me insights to discuss with clients instead of just raw data dumps.

But you need to be careful about AI hallucinations and errors. AI tools are confident even when they're wrong, and they'll generate plausible-sounding but completely incorrect information without any warning. Never trust AI output without verification, especially for technical implementations or client-facing deliverables.

I learned this during a project where I used AI to generate database queries for a financial reporting system. The queries looked correct and ran without errors, but they were pulling data from the wrong tables and producing subtly incorrect results. It took two days of debugging to find and fix the problems.

Now I treat AI-generated code and analysis as first drafts that require thorough review and testing. The AI saves time on the initial creation, but I still need to validate everything before it goes into production or gets delivered to clients.

Client disclosure about AI use is essential and should be covered in your statement of work. Some clients are enthusiastic about AI and want to know how you're using it to improve efficiency. Others are concerned about data privacy, accuracy, or job displacement and prefer traditional approaches.

I include a section in my SOW that covers AI tool usage: "Consultant may use artificial intelligence tools to improve project efficiency for tasks covering code generation, documentation creation, and data analysis. All AI-generated content will be reviewed, validated, and customized before delivery. Client data will only be processed through AI tools with appropriate privacy and security protections."

This language gives me flexibility to use AI where appropriate while assuring clients that I'm not just passing through raw AI output as finished work. It also opens the door for conversations about AI applications that might benefit their project.

Some clients have strict policies against AI use, especially in regulated industries like healthcare and finance. Government contracts often prohibit AI tools entirely. Always check client policies before using any AI assistance, and be prepared to work without AI if required.

Data privacy becomes more complex when using AI tools. Most commercial AI services process data on external servers, which may violate client confidentiality agreements or regulatory requirements. Look for AI tools that offer local processing or have strong data protection guarantees.

I use different AI tools depending on the sensitivity of the data involved. For public information or generic tasks, cloud-based AI services work fine. For confidential client data, I use local AI tools or services with explicit data protection agreements.

Quality control requires more attention when using AI. You need processes to verify AI output and catch errors before they reach clients. This covers code testing, fact-checking, and review by human experts who understand the domain.

I've developed checklists for different types of AI-generated content. Code gets run through automated testing and manual review. Documentation gets fact-checked against source materials and reviewed for client accuracy. Data analysis gets validated through alternative methods or spot-checking.

AI can create competitive advantages if used strategically. Projects that would have taken weeks can be completed in days. Routine tasks that consumed billable hours can be automated, freeing time for higher-value consulting activities. Clients benefit from faster delivery and often better quality outputs.

But AI can also commoditize certain types of consulting work. If your value proposition is based solely on tasks that AI can automate, you need to evolve your service offering or risk being displaced by cheaper alternatives.

I've shifted my focus toward activities that require human judgment, client relationship management, and complex problem-solving. AI handles the routine implementation work while I concentrate on strategy, architecture, and stakeholder management.

Training and staying current with AI tools is an ongoing investment. The technology evolves rapidly, with new capabilities and tools appearing constantly. What's new today might be obsolete next year. Budget time for learning and experimentation.

I spend a few hours each month testing new AI tools and techniques. Not everything proves useful, but the experimentation helps me identify tools that can improve project efficiency or open up new service opportunities.

Pricing and billing can get complicated when AI cuts project time. If you're charging fixed prices based on traditional effort estimates, AI efficiency improvements go straight to your profit margin. If you're billing hourly, AI might reduce your revenue unless you find ways to add more value.

I've moved toward value-based pricing for projects where AI provides big efficiency gains. Instead of billing for the time saved by AI, I price based on the value delivered to the client. This allows me to capture some of the efficiency benefits while still providing cost savings to clients.

The ethical considerations around AI use extend beyond simple disclosure. You need to consider the impact on workers whose jobs might be displaced, the accuracy and bias of AI outputs, and the long-term implications of increasing AI dependence.

I'm transparent with clients about how AI is changing the consulting landscape and what it means for their internal teams. Sometimes this leads to conversations about AI training or strategy that become additional consulting opportunities.

AI integration should enhance your consulting practice, not replace your expertise. The most successful consultants I know use AI to handle routine tasks while focusing their human skills on complex problem-solving, relationship building, and strategic thinking.

Start small with AI adoption. Pick one routine task that you do regularly and experiment with AI assistance. Learn what works, what doesn't, and how to integrate AI tools into your workflow. Build expertise gradually instead of trying to revolutionize your entire practice overnight.

AI will not replace consultants who combine real expertise with strong client relationships. It will replace the ones who don't bother learning to use it. The technology is too useful to leave to your competitors.

The future belongs to consultants who can combine human expertise with AI capabilities. Start building those skills now, before the competitive landscape shifts even further.

| **22** |

Modern project management tools

The consulting world has been transformed by technology over the past decade. When I started out, project management meant Excel spreadsheets, email chains, and phone calls. Today, there are hundreds of tools designed to make collaboration easier, communication clearer, and projects more organized.

The challenge isn't finding tools. It's figuring out which ones add value and which ones just create more complexity. I've seen consultants spend more time managing their project management software than managing their projects.

My wake-up call came during a project for a software company that insisted on using their elaborate project management platform. This thing had Gantt charts, resource allocation matrices, dependency tracking, automated reporting, risk assessment modules, and about fifty other features I didn't need.

The CEO, a guy named Thornton, was obsessed with metrics and dashboards. He wanted real-time visibility into every aspect of the project. How many hours each team member worked each day. What percentage of tasks were completed on schedule. Which deliverables were at risk of being delayed.

I spent the first week just learning how to use their system. Creating a simple task required filling out twelve different fields. Updating project status took an hour every morning. Generating the weekly report that Thornton demanded took half a day.

Three weeks into the project, I was spending more time updating the project management system than doing the work. The tool that was supposed to make us more efficient was killing our productivity.

That's when I learned the most important rule about project management tools: they should simplify your work, not complicate it. If a tool requires training, generates busywork, or takes time away from the core project activities, it's probably the wrong tool.

Now I start every project with the simplest tools that will get the job done. For most projects, that means a combination of email, shared documents, and maybe one collaboration platform.

Email remains the backbone of project communication. Everyone knows how to use it, it works on every device, and it creates an automatic record of decisions and discussions. People who dismiss email as old-fashioned are usually trying to sell you something more complicated.

The key is using email effectively. I create separate email threads for different aspects of the project: technical discussions, client communications, team coordination, and administrative issues. This keeps conversations organized and makes it easy to find information later.

I also use clear, descriptive subject lines that include the project name and topic. "ProjectX - Database Design Questions" is much more useful than "Quick Question" when you're searching through six months of messages.

For document collaboration, shared cloud storage beats email attachments every time. Whether you use Google Drive, Dropbox, OneDrive, or something else doesn't matter much. What matters is having a single location where everyone can access the latest versions of project files.

I organize project folders with a consistent structure: requirements, design documents, development files, testing materials, and client deliverables. Everyone on the team knows where to find things and where to put new materials.

Version control becomes critical when multiple people are working on the same documents. Nothing kills productivity faster than discovering that three people have been editing different versions of the same specification. Cloud-based collaboration tools handle this automatically, but you still need to establish conventions about when to create new versions and how to name them.

For real-time communication, instant messaging fills the gap between email and phone calls. Slack, Microsoft Teams, and similar platforms let team members ask quick questions, share links, and coordinate activities without cluttering everyone's inbox.

The key is establishing guidelines about what belongs in instant messages versus email. Quick questions, status updates, and casual coordination work well in chat. Important decisions, detailed discussions, and anything that might be referenced later should go in email.

Video conferencing has become essential for remote teams and client meetings. The technology has improved dramatically over the past few years, and most platforms now provide reliable audio and video quality.

I've found that video calls work best for certain purposes: project kickoffs, requirements discussions, design reviews, and problem-solving sessions. They're not great for status updates or information sharing, which can be handled more efficiently through other channels.

The biggest mistake I see with video meetings is not having clear agendas and objectives. A 30-minute call with five people costs 2.5 hours of collective time. Make sure that investment produces results that justify the cost.

For complex projects that require formal project management, I use dedicated tools like Asana, Trello, or Monday.com. These platforms help track tasks, deadlines, dependencies, and progress without the overhead of enterprise-level tools.

The key is choosing a tool that matches your project's complexity. Simple projects need simple tools. Complex projects can justify more sophisticated platforms, but only if the team will use them consistently.

I learned this during a project for a healthcare company that wanted to implement a new patient management system. The project involved eight team members, twelve different deliverables, and integration with five existing systems. Email and shared folders weren't going to cut it.

We chose Asana because it provided task tracking, deadline management, and progress visibility without requiring extensive training. Team members could see what they needed to work on, when it was due, and how their work connected to other parts of the project.

The tool worked because it simplified project coordination instead of complicating it. Team members spent five minutes a day updating their tasks instead of an hour filling out status reports. I could see project progress at a glance instead of chasing people for updates.

File sharing and version control become more important as project teams grow. Small teams can get by with shared folders and naming conventions. Larger teams need more sophisticated approaches.

For software development projects, Git-based platforms like GitHub or GitLab provide industrial-strength version control with branching, merging, and change tracking. For document-heavy projects, platforms like SharePoint or Confluence offer workflow management and approval processes.

The important thing is establishing clear procedures before problems arise. Who has access to what files? How are changes reviewed and approved? What happens when someone needs to work offline? Address these questions early and document the answers.

Time tracking tools can provide valuable insights into project profitability and resource allocation. Toggl, RescueTime, and similar platforms make it easy to log hours against different tasks and projects.

I use time tracking selectively. For fixed-price projects, I track time to understand profitability and improve future estimates. For hourly projects, I track time to provide accurate billing and demonstrate value to clients.

The key is making time tracking as painless as possible. Tools that integrate with your other applications or provide one-click timers reduce friction and improve accuracy.

Reporting and analytics tools help communicate project status to stakeholders. Most project management platforms include built-in reporting, but sometimes you need custom dashboards or presentations.

I create simple status reports that focus on three things: what's been accomplished, what's coming next, and any issues that need attention. Fancy charts and metrics rarely add value unless the client requests them.

AI handles first-draft status reports well. Keep a running note during the week of what you accomplished, what's blocked, and what's next — bullet points are fine — then paste it into an AI tool and ask for a client-ready status update in your standard format. The output needs editing for tone and accuracy, but the structural work is done. For consultants who hate writing status reports, this removes the main friction. You still have to think about what happened; you just don't have to write it up from scratch.

The goal isn't to use the latest and greatest tools. It's to choose tools that make your team more productive and your clients happier. Start simple, add complexity only when it provides clear benefits, and always prioritize usability over features.

The best project management system is the one that your team uses consistently without complaining. If people are constantly finding workarounds or avoiding the tools, you've chosen poorly.

Pick a set of tools that work, learn them well, and stop shopping. The time you spend evaluating the next great platform is time you're not billing.

| **23** |

CRMs and business tools

The right business tools can transform your consulting practice from a chaotic collection of spreadsheets and sticky notes into a professional operation that scales efficiently. But the wrong tools can waste time and money while creating more problems than they solve. The key is choosing simple, integrated solutions that match your needs instead of impressive features you'll never use.

Most consultants either avoid business tools entirely or go overboard with complex systems that require more maintenance than the consulting work itself. I've seen consultants spend more time updating their project management software than managing projects, and others who track prospects in random notebooks and wonder why leads fall through the cracks.

I learned about business tools through trial and error during my first few years of consulting. I started with no systems at all, keeping client information in my head and tracking projects through email threads. This worked fine for one or two clients but became impossible as the business grew.

When I landed my first three simultaneous projects, everything fell apart. I double-booked meetings, lost track of project deadlines, forgot to follow up with prospects, and submitted invoices late because I couldn't remember what work had been completed. I realized I needed real business systems, not just good intentions.

I went overboard in the opposite direction and bought expensive software for everything: complex CRM systems, elaborate project management platforms, detailed time tracking tools, and sophisticated financial management software. Each tool required setup, training, and ongoing maintenance that ate into billable hours.

The complexity became overwhelming. I spent so much time entering data, generating reports, and maintaining integrations between systems that I had less time for consulting work. The tools were supposed to make me more efficient, but they were making me less productive.

That experience taught me that business tools should solve real problems, not create new ones. The best tools are simple enough to use consistently but powerful enough to grow with your business. Complexity for its own sake is counterproductive.

I landed on Zoho as my primary platform because it bundles CRM, project management, invoicing, and file storage in one system. That integration matters more than any individual feature — every time you have to copy data between separate tools, you introduce errors and waste time. HubSpot, Salesforce, and Monday.com are all reasonable alternatives depending on your budget and how many clients you're managing. The specific platform matters less than picking one and actually using it.

Customer relationship management is essential for any consulting practice beyond the single-client level. A CRM system tracks prospects through your sales pipeline, maintains contact information, documents communication history, and schedules follow-up activities. Without systematic prospect management, leads get lost and opportunities disappear.

The CRM doesn't need to be complex to be effective. Basic contact management, communication logging, and pipeline tracking cover most consulting needs. Advanced features like marketing automation and lead scoring are usually overkill for independent consultants who maintain personal relationships with all their prospects.

I use Zoho CRM for this, but HubSpot has a free tier that covers everything most independent consultants need, and Pipedrive is worth a look if you want something simpler. Whatever you choose, track every prospect from initial contact through project completion — basic information, communication history, project details, and next actions. The pipeline view should show you at a glance where each prospect stands and what needs to happen next.

The key is entering information consistently instead of trying to capture every detail. I log big conversations, record follow-up commitments, and update pipeline status after each interaction. This minimal discipline prevents prospects from falling through the cracks.

Project management tools help organize work, track progress, and coordinate with clients and team members. For consulting projects, you need task management, deadline tracking, file sharing, and communication tools. You don't need elaborate Gantt charts or resource allocation features designed for large organizations.

I use Zoho Projects, but Asana and Trello work just as well for most consulting projects and are easier for clients to get comfortable with quickly. Each project should get its own workspace with task lists, milestone tracking, document storage, and a communication thread. Give clients access so they can review progress and download deliverables without having to ask you for updates.

The project management approach should match your working style instead of forcing you to adapt to rigid methodologies. Some consultants prefer detailed task breakdowns with precise time estimates. Others work better with high-level milestones and flexible execution. Choose tools that support your natural project management approach.

Time tracking becomes important for hourly billing and project analysis. Accurate time records support client invoicing, help with future project estimation, and provide insights about which activities generate the most value. But time tracking can become obsessive if you're not careful about finding the right balance.

I track time at the project level instead of trying to account for every minute. I log blocks of time against major activities: client meetings, technical work, documentation, communication. This provides enough detail for billing and analysis without becoming a micromanagement burden.

If your project management tool has built-in time tracking — Zoho, Toggl, Harvest — use it. The real value is when time entries flow automatically into invoices, which eliminates a whole category of billing errors. Standalone time trackers work fine too, but you'll be copying numbers around manually.

Financial management tools handle invoicing, payment tracking, expense management, and financial reporting. For consulting businesses, you need professional-looking invoices, systematic payment follow-up, and clear financial visibility. You don't need complex accounting features designed for inventory-based businesses.

I use Zoho Books for invoicing and financial management. FreshBooks and QuickBooks are both solid alternatives — FreshBooks in particular is built for service businesses and is easier to learn than QuickBooks. Whatever you pick, the goal is the same: invoices generated from your time and project records, automated payment reminders, and expense tracking without manual data entry.

The invoicing process should be as automated as possible to ensure consistent billing and prompt payment. I set up invoice templates with standard terms and payment instructions. Time entries and project milestones trigger invoice generation automatically. Payment reminders go out systematically without manual intervention.

Communication tools become critical when working with remote clients and distributed team members. Email integration, video conferencing, and file sharing need to work smoothly together. But avoid the temptation to adopt every new communication platform that clients suggest.

I use a core set of communication tools and ask clients to work within that framework. Email for formal communications, Zoho for project collaboration, Zoom for video calls, and phone for urgent issues. Having standard communication channels reduces confusion and ensures nothing gets lost in multiple platforms.

File storage and sharing require systematic organization to prevent chaos as projects accumulate. Cloud-based storage with version control, access permissions, and search capabilities becomes essential for managing client documents and project deliverables.

Google Drive and SharePoint both handle this well and are already familiar to most clients. I use Zoho WorkDrive to keep everything in the same platform, but the platform matters less than the discipline: one folder per project, consistent naming, proper access controls so each client only sees their own files. Version management saves you when someone overwrites something at the wrong moment, and it will happen.

Marketing tools for consultants should focus on relationship management instead of mass marketing campaigns. Contact management, email newsletters, and social media integration support business development activities without overwhelming complexity.

For marketing outreach I use Zoho's built-in tools, but Mailchimp covers this at lower cost if you're not on an integrated platform. The content is more important than the tool: quarterly newsletters, occasional industry observations, holiday check-ins. Keep them brief and useful rather than promotional. Most email marketing platforms let you segment by client type or project history, which lets you send relevant content instead of blasting everyone with the same message.

Integration between tools matters more than individual feature sets. Data should flow automatically between CRM, project management, time tracking, and invoicing systems. Manual data entry between systems creates opportunities for errors and wastes time on administrative tasks.

Integration is the real argument for staying within one platform family rather than mixing and matching. When your CRM, project management, time tracking, and invoicing all share the same database, information flows without you copying it. If you go with separate best-of-breed tools, budget time for maintaining the connections between them — that overhead adds up.

Mobile access becomes important for consultants who work on-site with clients or travel frequently. The ability to update project status, log time, and access client information from mobile devices keeps business systems current regardless of location.

Most major platforms have decent mobile apps now. Whatever you choose, make sure you can log time, check project status, and pull up a client record from your phone. When you're on-site with a client or traveling, you shouldn't need a laptop to keep your records current.

Backup and security considerations become critical when business tools contain sensitive client information. Automatic backups, data encryption, and access controls protect both your business and client confidentiality. Don't overlook these fundamentals when evaluating business platforms.

Any major cloud platform — Zoho, HubSpot, Salesforce, Google Workspace — invests more in security infrastructure than you could afford to build yourself. Use one of them. The risk of self-hosted solutions with client data is not worth the marginal cost savings.

Cost considerations should cover both subscription fees and implementation time when evaluating business tools. Expensive platforms that require extensive setup and training might cost more than simple solutions that work adequately for consulting needs.

I prefer paying reasonable monthly fees for integrated platforms instead of trying to build custom solutions or manage multiple point solutions. The time saved on administration and integration usually justifies the subscription costs.

Training and adoption become critical success factors regardless of which tools you choose. The best software is worthless if you don't use it consistently. Start with basic features and gradually adopt advanced capabilities as they become relevant to your business.

Whatever platform you choose, implement it gradually rather than trying to migrate everything at once. I added Zoho in stages over several months — CRM first, then project management, then invoicing. Each addition had time to settle before the next one landed. Trying to overhaul all your systems simultaneously is a good way to end up abandoning all of them.

The goal of business tools is supporting your consulting practice, not becoming a second career in system administration. Choose simple, integrated solutions that solve real problems without creating new complexity. Your clients hire you for consulting expertise, not for maintaining elaborate business software.

| 24 |

Marketing yourself between projects

Marketing is the difference between a sustainable consulting practice and constantly scrambling for your next project. Most consultants are terrible at marketing because they think it's sleazy, time-consuming, or something they can ignore until they need work. By then, it's too late.

I learned this lesson during a dry spell that nearly ended my consulting career. I'd just finished a six-month project for a healthcare company and was feeling confident about my prospects. The project had gone well, the client was happy, and I had what I thought were several solid leads for follow-up work.

Then everything fell apart at once. The healthcare client's budget got frozen due to regulatory changes. Two other prospects decided to handle their projects internally. A third prospect disappeared entirely after their company got acquired. Within two weeks, I went from having too much work to having no work at all.

I figured I'd find something quickly. I had a good reputation, solid technical skills, and years of experience. I started reaching out to former clients, updated my LinkedIn profile, and posted my availability on a few freelancing websites.

Nothing happened. Weeks turned into months. My savings dwindled while I sent out proposals that went nowhere. I lowered my rates, expanded my service offerings, and applied for projects I was overqualified for. Still nothing.

That's when I realized I'd made a fundamental mistake. I'd been so focused on delivering good work for current clients that I'd completely neglected building a pipeline of future opportunities. When my current work ended, I had no marketing momentum to carry me forward.

The dry spell lasted eight months and nearly bankrupted me. I eventually landed a small project that led to bigger work, but the experience taught me that marketing isn't something you do when you need work. It's something you do constantly, especially when you don't need work.

Now I spend 10-15% of my time on marketing activities, even during the busiest project periods. This consistent investment keeps potential clients aware of my services and builds relationships that turn into projects months or years later.

The foundation of consulting marketing is reputation management. Everything you do either builds or damages your professional reputation. Good work, clear communication, and professional behavior build reputation. Poor work, missed deadlines, and difficult behavior destroy it.

Your reputation travels faster and farther than you realize. The consulting world is smaller than it appears, and people talk. A satisfied client tells colleagues about good consultants. An unhappy client tells everyone about bad ones. One project disaster can haunt you for years.

I focus on three core marketing activities: content creation, networking, and referral management. Each serves a different purpose and reaches different audiences, but together they create a comprehensive marketing program that generates consistent opportunities.

Content creation establishes you as an expert in your field and makes it easy for potential clients to find you. This doesn't mean becoming a full-time blogger or social media influencer. It means sharing your knowledge and insights in ways that demonstrate your expertise.

I write articles about database design challenges, speak at industry conferences about system integration best practices, and participate in online forums where potential clients ask technical questions. Each piece of content positions me as someone who understands the problems that my target clients face.

The key is consistency instead of volume. One thoughtful article per month is better than sporadic bursts of content followed by months of silence. Potential clients need to see regular evidence of your expertise and current involvement in your field.

LinkedIn has become the primary platform for B2B content marketing, especially for consultants. I post weekly updates about project challenges, industry trends, and technical insights. These posts keep me visible to my network and often generate direct inquiries from potential clients.

AI is genuinely useful for breaking through the blank-page problem on content. If you have a lesson from a recent project but can't figure out how to frame it as a post, describe it to an AI tool and ask for three different angles. You'll almost always find one that sparks something — then rewrite it in your own voice. The goal is a post that reads like you, not like a press release. AI can generate the structure; you provide the voice and the specific detail that makes the post worth reading. Generic AI content is immediately recognizable and does more damage to your credibility than posting nothing.

The content doesn't need to be groundbreaking or revolutionary. Practical tips, lessons learned from recent projects, and observations about industry changes all work well. The goal is demonstrating competence and staying top-of-mind with your professional network.

Speaking at conferences and industry events provides more credibility than any amount of online content. When you're introduced as an expert and speak to an audience of your peers, you establish authority that's difficult to achieve through other marketing channels.

I look for speaking opportunities at regional conferences, user group meetings, and professional association events. The topics usually come from challenges I've solved in recent consulting projects. A database migration that went well becomes a presentation about data migration best practices.

The speaking itself generates some leads, but the real value comes from the relationships you build with other attendees. Conference speakers are automatically positioned as experts, making it easier to start conversations and build professional connections.

Networking is about building relationships, not collecting business cards. The consultants who succeed at networking focus on being helpful to others instead of promoting themselves. When you help other people solve problems or make connections, they remember you when opportunities arise.

I attend local business groups, industry meetups, and professional association events. Instead of pitching my services, I listen for problems I might be able to help with and people I can connect with others in my network. This approach builds genuine relationships that often lead to referrals.

The key is consistency and authenticity. Show up regularly, be genuinely interested in helping others, and avoid the hard sell. People buy consulting services from people they know, like, and trust. Focus on building those relationships before you need them.

Online networking through LinkedIn and industry forums can be just as valuable as in-person events. I participate in discussion groups related to my consulting areas and try to provide helpful answers to technical questions. This builds recognition and demonstrates expertise to a broader audience.

Referral management is the most powerful marketing tool for consultants, but it requires systematic attention. Most consultants assume that satisfied clients will automatically refer new business. Some will, but many won't unless you make it easy and give them reasons to think of you.

I maintain regular contact with former clients through quarterly check-ins, industry updates, and holiday greetings. These touchpoints keep me visible and make it more likely they'll think of me when referral opportunities arise.

I also ask for referrals directly, but in a way that makes it easy for clients to help. Instead of saying "please refer me to other people," I say "I'm looking for companies that are struggling with inventory management systems. Do you know anyone who might benefit from that type of help?"

Testimonials and case studies provide social proof that makes referrals more effective. When former clients recommend your services, they can point to examples of your work and the results you achieved. This makes their referrals more credible and compelling.

I collect testimonials immediately after successful project completions, when client satisfaction is highest and the results are fresh in their minds. I also write brief case studies that highlight the challenges, solutions, and outcomes from interesting projects.

Online presence management has become essential as more clients research consultants online before making contact. Your website, LinkedIn profile, and search results need to present a professional image and make it easy for potential clients to understand your services.

My website focuses on the problems I solve instead of the technologies I use. Instead of saying "I provide database consulting services," I say "I help companies migrate from legacy systems to modern databases without losing critical data." This approach speaks to client needs instead of consultant capabilities.

Social media can support your marketing efforts, but it's not essential for most consulting practices. If you enjoy creating content and engaging online, LinkedIn is the platform that matters for B2B consulting. Other platforms may be relevant depending on your specialization, but LinkedIn is the one worth investing time in.

The key is authenticity and consistency. Share insights from your work, comment thoughtfully on industry developments, and engage with other professionals' content. Avoid controversial topics that might alienate potential clients, and remember that everything you post reflects on your professional reputation.

Email marketing to your professional network can be effective if done thoughtfully. I send quarterly updates to my contact list covering interesting projects, industry trends, and service updates. The emails are brief, informative, and focused on providing value instead of selling services.

The goal is staying visible and helpful instead of pushing for immediate business. When people in your network have consulting needs or know someone who does, they're more likely to think of you if you've been providing useful information regularly.

Marketing measurement for consultants is different from product marketing. You're not tracking clicks and conversion rates. You're building relationships and reputation that pay off months or years later. Track activities like content creation, networking events attended, and follow-up conversations instead of immediate sales results.

The most important metric is pipeline health: how many qualified prospects are you talking to at any given time? A healthy consulting practice has 3-5 active prospect conversations, even when you're busy with current projects.

Marketing timing is crucial for consultants because sales cycles are long and unpredictable. You need to start marketing for your next project while you're still working on your current one. The best time to look for work is when you don't need it.

Start marketing efforts immediately after landing a new project, when you have the confidence and credibility that comes from recent success. This momentum makes it easier to create content, attend networking events, and build relationships.

Remember that marketing is an investment in your long-term business success, not a cost to be minimized. The time and money you spend on marketing activities will pay dividends through better projects, higher rates, and more consistent work flow.

Consistent marketing effort is what separates successful consulting practices from feast-or-famine freelancers. Make marketing a regular part of your business routine, not something you do only when work runs out.

| 25 |

Testimonials, referrals, and recommendations

Testimonials and referrals are the lifeblood of consulting businesses, but most consultants wait too long to ask for them or never ask at all. The time to request testimonials is after the first milestone success or some other major project win, not at the end when clients feel like they don't owe you anything anymore.

I learned about testimonial timing during a database migration project for a regional bank. The first phase involved extracting and cleaning their customer data from a legacy system that had been causing problems for years. When we completed the extraction successfully and the client saw clean, usable data for the first time in months, they were ecstatic.

That was the perfect moment to ask for a testimonial, but I didn't think of it. I was focused on the technical work and assumed I'd ask for references when the entire project was finished. By the time we completed the final implementation three months later, the initial excitement had faded. The client was satisfied but not thrilled, and getting testimonials felt like pulling teeth.

The psychology of testimonials is simple: people are most enthusiastic about recommending you when they're experiencing the immediate benefits of your work. Early project successes create emotional highs where clients genuinely want to share their positive experience. Wait until the end, and that emotional peak has passed.

Now I ask for testimonials immediately after big milestones. When a client sees their first clean data report, when a system goes live successfully, when a critical integration works perfectly - those are the moments when testimonials write themselves because the value is obvious and immediate.

The timing conversation is straightforward. I might say, "I'm thrilled that the data extraction went so smoothly and you're seeing the quality improvements you needed. Would you be willing to write a brief testimonial about this phase of the project? It would really help other potential clients understand the value of proper data migration."

Most clients are happy to provide testimonials when they're asked at the right moment. They're experiencing real benefits from your work, they appreciate your expertise, and they want to help you succeed. The key is asking while that goodwill is at its peak instead of treating testimonials as an afterthought.

Ask for both LinkedIn recommendations and written testimonials. LinkedIn recommendations provide social proof on the platform where most business professionals research consultants. Written testimonials give you flexibility to use the content in proposals, on your website, and in marketing materials.

LinkedIn recommendations are valuable because they're attached to real profiles and can't be easily faked. When potential clients see that senior executives at recognizable companies have recommended your work, it provides credibility that generic testimonials can't match.

The request process for LinkedIn recommendations is simple. Send a request through LinkedIn's recommendation feature with a brief note explaining what you'd like them to highlight. LinkedIn also allows you to include a draft recommendation when you send the request, making the process even easier for your client.

Write a draft recommendation yourself and include it in the LinkedIn request. The client can then approve it as-is, make modifications, or write their own version. This approach removes the blank-page problem and ensures you get recommendations that highlight the results and benefits you want to emphasize.

Written testimonials give you more control over format and usage. You can include them in proposals, feature them on your website, and incorporate them into case studies. Ask for written testimonials in addition to LinkedIn recommendations, not instead of them.

Write the testimonials yourself and ask clients to approve them with changes. This might sound presumptuous, but it makes the process easier for everyone involved. Clients get a well-written testimonial that highlights the right points, and you get testimonials that focus on the benefits you want to emphasize.

Recommendations and testimonials should always discuss details where possible: deadlines met, goals achieved, problems solved, measurable improvements. Generic praise like "great to work with" or "highly recommend" tells potential clients nothing useful about your capabilities or the results you deliver.

A worthless testimonial reads: "Working with *Your Name* was great. Very professional and knowledgeable. Would definitely recommend."

A valuable testimonial reads: "Working with *Your Name* on our inventory system upgrade delivered exactly what we needed. The project was completed two weeks ahead of the original deadline, the new database structure reduced our monthly reporting time by 90%, and the automated alerts eliminated the stock-out problems that had been costing us revenue. The entire implementation stayed within budget."

The detailed testimonial tells potential clients exactly what you accomplished, how you performed against deadlines and budget, and what measurable business value you delivered. Percentages and relative improvements provide concrete evidence without revealing sensitive company information.

The draft testimonial should be written in the client's voice and highlight results or benefits from your work. Instead of generic praise, focus on measurable outcomes, problem resolution, or process improvements that other potential clients would find relevant.

Send the draft with a message like: "I've drafted a testimonial based on our conversations about the project results. Please feel free to modify this however you'd like, or if you prefer to write something completely different, that works too. I just wanted to make this as easy as possible for you."

Most clients appreciate having a starting point instead of facing a blank page. They'll often approve the draft with minor changes or use it as a template for writing their own version. The key is making the testimonial process effortless for them while ensuring you get content that effectively promotes your services.

By the end of the project, clients don't owe you anything beyond payment for completed work. The psychological dynamic shifts from gratitude for ongoing benefits to relief that the project is finished. Getting testimonials becomes much more difficult because clients have moved on mentally and emotionally.

I've seen consultants complete successful projects and then struggle for weeks to get simple testimonials from satisfied clients. The clients aren't being difficult - they're just focused on other priorities and don't feel the same urgency about helping with testimonials that they felt during active project phases.

The contrast is stark between testimonials requested during project highs versus testimonials requested after project completion. Early testimonials are enthusiastic and detailed. Late testimonials are generic and perfunctory, if you get them at all.

Referral requests follow the same timing principles as testimonials. The best time to ask for referrals is when clients are experiencing the benefits of your work, not months later when the project is a distant memory.

When asking for referrals, be clear about the types of clients you're looking for instead of making vague requests for "anyone who might need consulting." Something like: "I'm looking to help other manufacturing companies with similar inventory challenges. Do you know anyone who's struggling with stock management or reporting issues?"

Clear referral requests make it easier for clients to think of appropriate connections and give them language to use when making introductions. They can say, "I know someone who handles inventory system problems" instead of "I know a consultant who might be able to help with something."

The referral conversation should feel natural instead of transactional. Frame it as helping other companies solve problems similar to the ones you solved for them. Most clients are willing to help peers who face similar challenges, especially when they've had positive experiences with your solutions.

Case studies provide another way to use successful projects for future marketing. Ask permission to write case studies during project planning instead of waiting until the end. Clients are more likely to agree when they're excited about working with you than when they're wrapping up the engagement.

The case study request should cover how you'll handle confidentiality and what approval process you'll use. Something like: "I'd like to write a case study about this project to help other companies facing similar challenges. I'll anonymize any sensitive information and give you final approval before using it in any marketing materials."

Anonymous case studies still provide value for marketing purposes because they demonstrate your problem-solving approach and the types of results you achieve. Many clients are comfortable with anonymous case studies even if they wouldn't agree to named testimonials.

Video testimonials provide even more credibility than written testimonials, but they require more effort from clients. Save video testimonial requests for your best client relationships and most impressive project successes. The extra production effort is only worthwhile when you have truly exceptional results to showcase.

Testimonial and referral systems should be built into your project management process instead of handled ad hoc. Include testimonial requests in your project milestone templates. Set calendar reminders to ask for referrals during peak client satisfaction periods. Make relationship management a systematic part of your consulting practice.

The goal isn't to pester clients for endorsements but to capture their enthusiasm when it's genuine and beneficial for both parties. Clients who are thrilled with your work want to help you succeed. Your job is to make it easy for them to provide that help when they're most motivated to do so.

Good testimonials and referrals create positive feedback loops that make marketing easier and more effective. Instead of trying to convince prospects about your capabilities, you can let satisfied clients tell your story for you. But only if you ask for that help at the right time and in the right way.

Don't wait until projects are finished to think about testimonials and referrals. By then, the moment has passed, and you've missed your best opportunity to turn satisfied clients into enthusiastic advocates for your consulting practice.

| 26 |

International and cultural considerations

Working with international clients opens up massive opportunities but creates challenges that can destroy projects if you're not prepared. Cultural misunderstandings, time zone complications, payment difficulties, and legal complexities multiply the normal risks of consulting work.

I learned about international consulting the hard way during a project with a German manufacturing company that wanted to implement a supply chain management system. The technical requirements were clear, my expertise was relevant, and the budget was generous. What I didn't anticipate was how cultural differences would turn a straightforward project into a six-month diplomatic nightmare.

The first warning sign came during our initial video conference. I started the meeting with casual small talk about the weather and weekend plans, normal for American business conversations. The German project manager looked uncomfortable and quickly steered the discussion to technical requirements. I thought he was just focused and efficient.

As the project progressed, I realized that my American communication style was creating problems. I would say things like "I think this approach might work" or "We should probably consider this option," intended as collaborative discussion. The German team interpreted this uncertainty as incompetence and lack of confidence in my recommendations.

They expected definitive statements backed by solid analysis. When I said "I think," they heard "I'm not sure." When I said "probably," they heard "maybe." My attempt to be collaborative came across as wishy-washy and unprofessional.

The cultural miscommunication reached a breaking point during a design review meeting. I presented three possible database architectures and asked for their input on the approach they preferred. The technical lead got frustrated and said, "You are the expert. Tell us the correct solution, not ask us to choose."

I realized I had been approaching the project with American expectations about collaborative decision-making and iterative feedback. The German culture values expertise, authority, and decisive recommendations. They hired me to make technical decisions, not to run group discussions about options.

Once I understood the cultural expectations, I changed my communication style. Instead of presenting options, I recommended solutions with supporting rationale. Instead of asking for input, I explained my decisions and asked for approval. The project relationship improved immediately, and we completed the implementation successfully.

That experience taught me that cultural differences go far beyond language barriers. Business practices, communication styles, decision-making processes, and relationship expectations vary dramatically between cultures. Assuming everyone operates like your domestic clients is a recipe for disaster.

Time zone management becomes a major operational challenge when working with international clients. A simple status meeting becomes a complex scheduling puzzle when team members are spread across continents. Someone always gets stuck with inconvenient meeting times, and important decisions get delayed because key people can't participate in real-time discussions.

I've learned to structure international projects around asynchronous communication whenever possible. Instead of trying to get everyone on the same call, I use detailed email updates, shared documentation, and recorded video presentations. This allows team members to participate at convenient times while maintaining project momentum.

For decisions that require real-time discussion, I rotate meeting times so that different team members take turns with early morning or late evening calls. I also record important meetings so that people who can't attend can review the discussion and provide input later.

Time zone differences can work in your favor if you plan properly. When I finish work at 6 PM Pacific time, my colleagues in India are starting their day. I can hand off work in the evening and have results waiting when I check email in the morning. This creates a 24-hour work cycle that can accelerate project timelines if managed well.

Communication preferences vary between cultures and can affect project success if not understood properly. Some cultures prefer formal, written communications with detailed documentation. Others favor informal verbal discussions with minimal paperwork. Some value direct feedback and open debate. Others consider direct criticism to be disrespectful and prefer indirect suggestions.

I research cultural business practices before engaging with international clients and ask local contacts about appropriate communication protocols. This covers understanding hierarchy expectations, meeting etiquette, and decision-making processes. Small cultural missteps can damage relationships and create obstacles that persist throughout the project.

Language barriers create obvious challenges, but the real problems often come from subtle misunderstandings instead of complete communication failures. Technical terms may not translate precisely between languages, and concepts that seem clear in English might have different implications in other languages.

I've learned to confirm understanding frequently during international projects and to document important decisions in writing.

When discussing complex technical concepts, I use diagrams, screenshots, and examples to supplement verbal explanations. I also ask team members to summarize key points in their own words to ensure we have shared understanding.

Legal and regulatory differences between countries can create unexpected complications for international projects. Data privacy laws, employment regulations, contract enforcement mechanisms, and dispute resolution processes vary dramatically between jurisdictions. What's legal and standard practice in one country might be prohibited or problematic in another.

I always research local legal requirements before taking on international projects and often consult with attorneys who understand both jurisdictions. This is especially important for projects involving personal data, financial information, or regulated industries like healthcare and banking.

Payment mechanics get complicated fast. Require advance payment for all international projects — this is non-negotiable, not a preference. Quote in US dollars to eliminate currency risk, or include currency adjustment clauses if the client insists on their local currency. Wire transfers from foreign banks trigger additional scrutiny from US banks; maintain a relationship with a bank that handles international business regularly. Get a tax advisor who works with international consultants before you sign your first cross-border contract. Different countries have different rules about when foreign consultants owe local taxes, and tax treaties between countries affect withholding in ways that will surprise you. One expensive surprise early in your international career will pay for years of good tax advice.

Contract enforcement across borders is harder than domestically. Collecting from an international client who refuses to pay is expensive and slow — legal remedies that work in the US often don't translate. The answer is larger advance payments and dispute resolution clauses that specify jurisdiction and applicable law upfront, before anyone is angry.

On the logistics side: visa requirements, holiday schedules, and technology infrastructure differences all need to be scoped before you commit to a timeline. A project timeline that looks reasonable on paper can fall apart when you discover your client is unavailable for three weeks due to local holidays you didn't know about, or that remote access to their systems requires VPN configurations that take two weeks to approve. Test connectivity before you promise delivery dates. Build buffer for travel delays and time zone friction. Research local business customs — gift-giving, meeting etiquette, and dress codes vary significantly and the wrong move creates friction that lingers.

International consulting can be extremely rewarding both financially and personally. The global market for consulting services is much larger than any domestic market, and some international clients are willing to pay premium rates for expertise that's not available locally. The cultural exchange and professional growth that comes from international work is also valuable.

But international consulting requires careful preparation, cultural sensitivity, and risk management. Start with smaller projects to learn the challenges before taking on major international engagements. Invest in understanding cultural differences and legal requirements. Build relationships with local partners who can help navigate cultural and business practices.

International clients can be some of the best you'll ever work with, and some of the most complicated. Do your homework on the cultural and legal differences before you sign anything, not after.

The world is full of clients who need consulting expertise, but success in international markets requires adapting your approach to different cultural and business environments.

| 27 |

Your website and online presence

Every consultant needs both a professional website and a complete LinkedIn profile. These aren't optional marketing extras - they're basic business requirements that potential clients expect to find when researching your services. Without proper online presence, you look unprofessional and lose credibility before prospects even contact you.

I learned about online presence importance when I lost a potential client because they couldn't find information about my services online. The prospect had been referred to me by a former client, but when they searched for my business, they found only a basic LinkedIn profile with minimal information and no dedicated website.

The prospect called my referral source and said they were concerned about working with someone who "didn't seem to have a real business presence online." They hired a competitor who had a professional website with case studies, service descriptions, and client testimonials. I lost a $50,000 project because I looked less credible than someone with better online presentation.

That experience taught me that online presence isn't about marketing sophistication - it's about basic professional credibility. Potential clients research consultants online before making contact, and poor online presence creates doubt about your professionalism and business stability.

Now I maintain both a professional website and a comprehensive LinkedIn profile that work together to provide complete information about my services, experience, and expertise. These platforms serve different purposes but reinforce the same professional message.

Your website serves as your business headquarters online. It provides detailed information about your services, demonstrates your expertise through case studies and content, and gives prospects confidence that you're a legitimate business professional. The website doesn't need to be elaborate, but it needs to be professional and informative.

The essential website content covers services offered, relevant experience, client testimonials, contact information, and examples of your work. Potential clients want to understand what you do, how you've helped similar companies, and why they should trust you with their projects.

Service descriptions should be clear and focused on client benefits instead of technical features. Instead of saying "I provide database optimization services," explain "I help companies reduce report generation time and improve data accuracy through database performance improvements." The focus should be on solving client problems, not showcasing technical skills.

Experience summaries should highlight relevant projects and industries without violating client confidentiality. You can describe the types of problems you've solved and the results you've achieved without naming clients or revealing sensitive information. Anonymous case studies work well for demonstrating capabilities.

Client testimonials provide third-party validation of your expertise and professionalism. Include testimonials that highlight different aspects of your services: technical competence, project management skills, communication quality, and business results. Make sure testimonials include details instead of generic praise.

Contact information should be prominent and complete. Include phone number, email address, and business location if relevant. Make it easy for prospects to reach you when they're ready to discuss their projects. Consider including a contact form for prospects who prefer that approach.

Simple website options work better than complex custom designs for most consultants. You don't need elaborate functionality or sophisticated design - you need clear information presentation and professional appearance. Focus on content quality instead of technical complexity.

WordPress on hosting platforms like SiteGround provides flexibility and professional appearance without requiring technical expertise. WordPress themes handle the design and layout while you focus on content creation. Hosting platforms provide technical support and handle software updates automatically.

Site builders like GoDaddy Website Builder or Wix offer even simpler approaches with drag-and-drop interfaces and built-in hosting. These platforms limit customization options but eliminate technical complexity entirely. You can create professional-looking websites without any technical knowledge.

The choice between WordPress and site builders depends on your technical comfort level and customization needs. WordPress offers more flexibility but requires more technical involvement. Site builders are simpler but more limited in functionality. Either approach can create effective consultant websites.

LinkedIn is where most B2B consulting prospects do their research, and your profile needs to hold up to that scrutiny. The headline is what they see first — "Database Consultant" tells them nothing. "I help manufacturing companies reduce reporting time and improve data accuracy" tells them exactly what you do and who you do it for. The same logic applies to your summary and experience sections: write about results, not job duties. "Led inventory system upgrade" is forgettable. "Reduced monthly close time from 12 days to 3 by replacing a legacy inventory system for a regional manufacturer" is memorable and searchable.

LinkedIn recommendations are the most credible thing on your profile because they can't be faked. Chase them systematically using the same approach covered in Chapter 25 — ask right after a project win, provide a draft, make it easy. A profile with ten detailed recommendations from recognizable companies beats a polished profile with none.

Post content on LinkedIn occasionally — a lesson from a recent project, an observation about something changing in your field, a short take on a problem you keep seeing. You don't need to post daily or build a personal brand. You need enough activity that when a prospect looks at your profile after a referral, they see someone who is currently working and thinking, not someone whose last update was two years ago. One solid post per month is enough to maintain that signal.

Use a professional headshot on both your website and LinkedIn — the same one, so you look consistent. Get a domain name that matches your business name and an email address on that domain. Gmail and Yahoo addresses on a consulting proposal undermine everything else you've built. Website hosting runs less than $100 per year. A professional email address costs about the same. These are the cheapest credibility signals available to you, and skipping them is a mistake I've seen cost people projects worth ten times that.

The goal of your online presence is making it easy for qualified prospects to find you, understand your services, and contact you about their projects. Everything else is secondary to those basic objectives.

Your website and LinkedIn profile work together to create professional credibility that supports your consulting business. Invest the time needed to create professional online presence, and you'll attract better clients who take your services seriously from the first interaction.

| 28 |

The end of the project

Ending consulting projects properly is just as important as starting them well. How you handle project closure affects client satisfaction, payment collection, future opportunities, and your professional reputation. Most consultants focus on delivering the final work and forget about the relationship management aspects of project completion.

I learned about project endings during my first major implementation for a healthcare company. The technical work went smoothly, all deliverables were completed on schedule, and the client was happy with the results. I submitted my final invoice, packed up my equipment, and moved on to the next project without much ceremony.

Three months later, the client called with questions about the system I'd implemented. They were having minor issues that weren't bugs but required someone familiar with the architecture to explain. I spent an hour on the phone walking them through the solutions, but the conversation felt awkward because I hadn't established any ongoing support arrangements.

Six months after that, the client started a new project that would have been perfect for my expertise. They hired a different consultant because they assumed I wasn't available or interested in additional work. I had delivered excellent technical results but failed to maintain the relationship after project completion.

That experience taught me that project endings are relationship transitions, not just delivery milestones. How you handle the transition affects whether clients become long-term advocates for your business or just satisfied customers who move on to other consultants.

Now I plan project endings as carefully as project beginnings. The final phase includes knowledge transfer, documentation handover, relationship maintenance planning, and future opportunity discussions. These activities take additional time but generate long-term value that far exceeds the investment.

Knowledge transfer ensures that client teams can maintain and support the work you've delivered. This isn't just about providing documentation, it's about making sure the right people understand how to operate, troubleshoot, and modify the systems or processes you've implemented.

I schedule formal knowledge transfer sessions during the final weeks of projects. These sessions cover system architecture, operational procedures, troubleshooting guides, and future enhancement possibilities. The goal is giving client teams enough understanding to handle routine issues without needing to call you for help.

Documentation handover goes beyond the technical documentation created during the project. I provide a complete project archive that includes contracts, communications, decision records, and all working files. This archive helps clients understand the project history and provides reference material for future modifications.

The documentation package also includes a project summary that highlights key decisions, lessons learned, and recommendations for future improvements. This summary serves as institutional memory that persists even when team members change roles or leave the organization.

Relationship maintenance planning involves identifying the key stakeholders who might influence future opportunities and establishing protocols for staying in touch. This isn't about pestering former clients with sales calls, it's about maintaining professional relationships that benefit both parties.

I create a contact schedule that includes quarterly check-ins with primary contacts, annual relationship reviews with key stakeholders, and ongoing communication through industry events or professional networks. These touchpoints keep relationships active without being intrusive.

Future opportunity discussions happen naturally during project wrap-up when clients are thinking about next steps and additional needs. The end of one project often reveals requirements for related work or highlights problems that weren't addressed in the original scope.

I use final project meetings to discuss potential follow-up work, but I frame these conversations around client needs rather than my desire for additional revenue. Something like: "Now that this system is in place, you might want to consider integrating it with your reporting platform. That's not urgent, but it could provide additional value when you're ready."

Payment collection becomes critical during project closure because this is often when final invoices are submitted and when clients feel like the business relationship is ending. Delayed payment on final invoices can create cash flow problems and damage relationships.

I submit final invoices promptly and follow up on payment status more aggressively than I do during active project phases. Clients who are transitioning to new priorities might not prioritize paying consultants who are no longer actively working on their problems.

Post-project support arrangements need to be established before projects end, not after problems arise. Some clients want ongoing maintenance agreements, others prefer ad hoc support, and some prefer to handle everything internally after knowledge transfer.

I discuss support preferences during project planning and confirm arrangements during project closure. Clear support agreements prevent misunderstandings about availability, response times, and billing arrangements when future issues arise.

The support conversation might cover warranty periods for delivered work, response time commitments for different types of issues, and billing arrangements for post-project assistance. Having these agreements in place makes future interactions smoother for everyone involved.

Success celebration might seem trivial, but it's an important part of project closure that many consultants skip. Taking time to acknowledge project achievements and thank team members creates positive memories that influence future opportunities.

I organize brief celebration meetings or send thank-you notes that highlight specific contributions and achievements. These gestures cost little but create goodwill that pays dividends in referrals and repeat business.

Lessons learned documentation helps improve future projects and provides valuable insights for both consultants and clients. I conduct brief post-mortem discussions that cover what worked well, what could have been improved, and what insights might apply to future projects.

These discussions aren't blame sessions or problem-solving meetings, they're learning opportunities that help everyone involved do better work in the future. The insights often lead to process improvements that benefit subsequent projects.

Reference establishment should happen during project closure while client satisfaction is highest and project details are fresh in everyone's memory. I ask for permission to use clients as references and confirm their willingness to discuss the project with potential clients.

The reference conversation includes discussing which aspects of the project they're comfortable discussing and which topics they'd prefer to avoid. Some clients are happy to discuss technical details but prefer not to talk about budget or timeline issues.

Client evaluation feedback helps improve your consulting practice and provides valuable insights about client satisfaction. I send brief evaluation surveys that cover project management, communication quality, technical delivery, and overall satisfaction.

The evaluation questions focus on practical feedback rather than generic satisfaction ratings. Instead of asking "How satisfied were you with communication?" I ask "What communication improvements would have been most helpful during this project?"

Transition planning helps clients move from active project mode to operational mode. This includes identifying who takes ownership of different system components, establishing maintenance schedules, and planning for future enhancements or modifications.

The transition plan should be documented and reviewed with all relevant stakeholders to ensure everyone understands their ongoing responsibilities. Clear transition planning prevents confusion and reduces the likelihood of post-project problems.

Professional development discussions can benefit both consultants and clients by identifying skills or knowledge that would be valuable for future projects. These conversations often reveal training opportunities or certification programs that could improve project outcomes.

I might suggest that client team members attend specific training programs or obtain certifications that would help them maintain the systems we've implemented. These recommendations demonstrate ongoing interest in their success beyond the current project.

Network expansion happens naturally during project closure when you've worked closely with client teams and built professional relationships. Project team members often move to other organizations where they might need similar consulting services.

I connect with key team members on LinkedIn and maintain professional relationships that extend beyond the specific project. These network connections often lead to opportunities at their future employers or referrals to their professional contacts.

Portfolio development involves documenting the project for future marketing use while the details are fresh and client feedback is available. This includes creating case studies, collecting testimonials, and photographing or documenting deliverables that can be show-cased to future clients.

The portfolio documentation process should respect client confidentiality while capturing the essential elements that demonstrate your capabilities to potential clients. Many clients are comfortable with anonymous case studies even if they prefer not to be named references.

Project closure checklists help ensure that nothing important gets overlooked during the transition from active work to project completion. These checklists cover all the activities mentioned above plus administrative tasks like final billing, file archiving, and contract completion.

I maintain detailed closure checklists that get customized for each project based on client needs and project characteristics. The checklist approach ensures consistent professional closure regardless of project pressure or competing priorities.

Remember that project endings are beginnings of long-term professional relationships. The impression you leave during project closure influences how clients remember you, whether they recommend you to others, and whether they hire you for future work.

Invest the time and effort needed to end projects professionally, and you'll build a consulting practice based on long-term client relationships rather than one-time transactions.

| **29** |

AI consulting as a service offering

Every organization in the country is trying to figure out what to do with artificial intelligence right now, and most of them have no idea where to start. That's not an insult — it's an accurate description of the current situation. The technology moved fast, the hype moved faster, and executives are sitting in board meetings fielding questions about their "AI strategy" while their teams are still figuring out whether to use the free version or pay for the subscription.

This is a consulting opportunity. Not just for technology consultants — for every type of consultant. HR consultants, marketing consultants, operations consultants, financial advisors, training specialists, process improvement experts. If your clients are organizations, they need help with AI. They just don't always know how to ask for it, and they're deeply skeptical of anyone who claims to have all the answers.

The most important thing to understand about AI consulting is that what clients actually need isn't what they think they need. They think they need someone to tell them which AI tools to buy. What they actually need is someone to help them figure out what problems they're solving, whether AI is the right tool for those problems, and what the realistic outcomes look like. That's a business consulting problem, not a technology problem. The technology is almost secondary.

I've watched organizations spend six figures on AI tools they don't use, run pilot programs that produce no measurable results, and task their IT departments with "implementing AI" without anyone having defined what success looks like. The problem in every case wasn't the technology. It was that nobody had done the basic consulting work first — understanding the actual workflows, identifying where the friction was, setting measurable goals, and thinking through what happens to the people whose jobs change when the AI gets deployed.

That work is what consultants do. You already know how to scope a project, interview stakeholders, document current processes, identify gaps, and write a recommendation that a client can actually act on. Apply those skills to AI and you're already ahead of most of the vendors pitching AI solutions, who are excellent at demonstrating what their products can do and useless at helping clients figure out whether they should buy them.

The entry point for most AI consulting engagements is what I call an AI readiness assessment. This is a structured discovery project — typically two to four weeks — where you audit the client's current operations, identify the workflows where AI could plausibly save time or reduce errors, assess whether their data is in good enough shape to support AI tools, evaluate their staff's comfort with new technology, and produce a prioritized roadmap of where to start. You're not building anything. You're not deploying anything. You're doing what good consultants do: helping the client understand their own situation clearly enough to make a good decision.

This type of engagement is well-suited to non-technical consultants because the hard questions aren't technical. They're things like: which of your customer service reps spend most of their day answering the same twenty questions? What does your document review process look like, and how many hours a week does it consume? Where do new employees get stuck in their first ninety days because the knowledge they need is locked in someone's head instead of written down? These are organizational and operational questions. The answer to "could AI help with this" usually becomes obvious once the question is framed correctly.

The follow-on engagements depend on your background. If you come from an HR background, you might help clients redesign job descriptions and performance management processes for a world where AI handles certain tasks that used to be part of those roles. If you're a marketing consultant, you might help them build content workflows that use AI for first drafts while preserving human judgment for strategy and brand voice. If you're an operations consultant, you might scope and oversee an AI implementation project without doing the technical work yourself — managing the vendor, setting success metrics, and making sure the rollout doesn't blow up the workflows it was supposed to improve.

Pricing AI consulting requires some care. The temptation is to charge a premium because the word "AI" is in the engagement title. Resist that. Clients are already suspicious that they're being oversold on AI, and an inflated rate will confirm their suspicions before you've had a chance to demonstrate value. Price based on the scope of work and the value delivered, same as any other engagement. An AI readiness assessment that saves a fifty-person company from spending $200,000 on the wrong tools should be priced on that value, not on a technology premium. Once you've delivered that assessment, the follow-on work prices itself.

The SOW for AI consulting needs two things that standard SOWs often skip. First, explicit scope around what you are and aren't providing — you're advising on strategy and process, not warranting that any specific AI tool will work as advertised, and not providing technical implementation unless that's separately scoped. Second, a clear statement about the limitations of AI predictions. The technology is changing fast enough that any roadmap you produce is a starting point, not a guarantee. Build that into the language so clients understand they're buying your expertise and judgment, not a promise about how the technology will behave six months from now.

The ethical dimension of AI consulting is real and worth taking seriously. When you help an organization implement AI tools that reduce the headcount needed for certain tasks, you're participating in a decision that affects people's jobs. That doesn't mean you shouldn't do it — organizations are going to make these changes with or without good consulting help, and better-guided implementations generally cause less unnecessary disruption than poorly-guided ones. But it means you should be honest with clients about the workforce implications of what they're planning, make sure they've thought through change management, and decline engagements where the real goal is to automate people out of jobs without any plan for how those people are treated in the process. That's your call to make, and you don't have to take every project that presents itself.

Stay current but don't chase every development. The AI landscape is producing new tools and capabilities constantly, and it's easy to spend all your time reading about AI instead of doing consulting work. You need enough familiarity to have credible conversations with clients and evaluate what's useful versus what's hype. You don't need to be an expert on every new model release. The consultants who are doing well in this space aren't the ones who know the most about the technology — they're the ones who know how to help organizations change, and who are applying that skill to a new category of problems.

Every organization is at the beginning of a long process of figuring out what AI means for how they operate. That process is going to require outside help. Whether that help comes from someone with a technology background or an operations background or an HR background matters less than whether it comes from someone who knows how to listen to what a client actually needs, scope work honestly, and deliver results they can measure. That's the work this entire book has been about. AI consulting is just one more place to apply it.

| 30 |

Conclusion

I want to go back to something from the Introduction for a moment. My first consulting gig was a $600 job fixing bugs in a general ledger program running on a TRS-80. I was overconfident, underprepared, and had no idea what I was doing. I didn't write a statement of work. I didn't validate my assumptions. I didn't have a contract that would have protected either of us. I had my eye on the $600 and ignored every warning sign until I was in too deep to back out gracefully.

I eventually fixed the bugs. I got paid. The client probably wondered why it took so long.

More than forty years and several hundred projects later, I still think about that first job. Not because it was a disaster — it wasn't, really — but because it was the clearest possible demonstration of something I had to learn the hard way: the technical work is never the problem. The business of consulting is the problem. Knowing how to fix a program is table stakes. Knowing how to scope the project, protect yourself legally, price your time correctly, and manage the relationship from kickoff to final invoice — that's the job.

Every story in this book — Randy losing two years of profits to a rounding error he wasn't insured for, Derek absorbing scope changes until the client blamed him for the whole mess, the regional bank where a $200/hour reviewer rubber-stamped my work while I ground through six weeks of implementation for less money than he made in a week — those aren't cautionary tales about incompetent consultants. Those are what happens to competent consultants who didn't treat the business side of consulting as seriously as the technical side.

The good news is that none of this is complicated once you've seen it clearly. Price based on value, not time. Get paid before you work. Write everything down. Don't work for free. Walk away from clients who won't respect the engagement. Get E&O insurance before you need it. Know who you're dealing with before you sign anything.

These aren't advanced concepts. They're just things nobody tells you when you're starting out — which is why I wrote this book in the first place. The first edition got adopted at Purdue's Krannert School of Management, which I'll never quite get over, but the audience I had in mind when I wrote it was myself at twenty years old, sitting in front of a TRS-80 with a $600 check on the line and no idea what I was getting into.

If this book saves you from making the expensive mistakes I made, it's done its job. If it helps you build a practice that pays you what you're worth and lets you work with clients who deserve your exper-tise, even better.

Now go fix their bugs. Just write the SOW first.

| 31 |

About the Author

Richard Lowe brings 40+ years of real-world experience to consulting guidance, built through decades of hands-on project management, client relationships, and business development across multiple industries. As someone who has lived through the challenges covered in this book - from pricing disasters to difficult clients to cash flow crises - his advice comes from the trenches, not from theory.

His consulting career spans Fortune 500 technology implementations, startup advisory work, and independent practice development. During 20 years as Director of Computer Operations at Trader Joe's, he managed technology projects supporting $16 billion in annual revenue while overseeing teams, budgets, and vendor relationships that taught him the business fundamentals essential for consulting success.

Richard's project management experience covers leading digital transformations for major retail operations, implementing SCADA systems for water utilities, developing fraud detection systems for telecommunications companies, and managing disaster recovery operations. These projects taught him how to handle scope creep, manage stakeholder expectations, navigate corporate politics, and deliver results under pressure - skills that translate directly to independent consulting success.

His database and systems expertise has been validated through academic recognition, with his book "How to Manage a Consulting Project" adopted as required reading at Purdue University's Krannert

School of Management. Professor Richard Makadok's endorsement reflects the practical value of his guidance: "This book helped my students avoid many subtle pitfalls in their client relationships."

The consulting principles in this book are proven through Richard's own practice, where he has successfully navigated the transition from corporate employment to independent consulting, built sustainable client relationships, and developed systems that support long-term business growth. His approach emphasizes practical execution over theoretical frameworks, focusing on the business fundamentals that determine whether consultants succeed or struggle.

Richard maintains an active consulting practice while writing extensively about business development, project management, and professional services. His direct experience with the challenges faced by independent consultants - from pricing strategies to difficult clients to international projects - provides the foundation for the practical guidance in this book.

You can learn more about Richard's consulting experience and ghostwriting services at *thewritingking.com* or connect with him on LinkedIn by searching Richard G. Lowe Jr.

BOOKS BY RICHARD LOWE

See books by Richard Lowe at
https://masterofworlds.com

Get free publishing insights and industry updates at
https://thewritingking.substack.com

For ghostwriting and book coaching services see
https://thewritingking.com